Architectural
Atmospheres

Architectural
Atmospheres
On the Experience and Politics
of Architecture

Christian Borch (Ed.)

With texts by
Gernot Böhme
Christian Borch
Olafur Eliasson
Juhani Pallasmaa

Birkhäuser
Basel

Contents

Christian Borch

**Introduction:
Why Atmospheres?**

Like any other social phenomenon, architecture reflects fads and fashions. Although trends do not shift as fast as in, for example, the clothing industry, certain architectural styles rise to prominence at certain times and in particular contexts, only to be replaced by other trends and fashions. One of the most significant recent trends is a turn towards (or perhaps a return to) atmospheric qualities in debates on architecture and urban space, as well as in practical architectural work. This is not to suggest that all architecture today revolves around atmospheric dimensions – it certainly, and regrettably, does not. Nevertheless, there seems to be a tendency for architects and urban planners to take seriously the atmospheric features of spatial design. One notable example of this is the Swiss architect Peter Zumthor, who was awarded the prestigious Pritzker Architecture Prize (commonly referred to as the Nobel Prize in architecture) in 2009. Zumthor is renowned for his explicit articulation of atmospheric concerns, as is manifest, for instance, in his book *Atmospheres: Architectural Environments, Surrounding Objects* (2006). In it, Zumthor reflects upon what constitutes quality in architecture. Why is it that some buildings feel more comfortable, pleasurable, and/or exciting than others? The answer, for Zumthor, lies in their atmospheric merits. It is the particular atmosphere of a building that moves us and hence endows it with architectural quality (2006: 11).

But to what, then, do atmospheres refer – and, more precisely, how do they move us? According to Zumthor – and his account is tightly linked to his work as a practising architect – two things are important. One relates to how we perceive or experience spaces. Thus, he asserts, '[w]e perceive atmosphere through our emotional sensibility – a form of perception that works incredibly quickly' (2006: 13). In essence, this amounts to some form of 'immediate appreciation, of a spontaneous emotional response': 'I enter a building, see a room, and – in the fraction of a second – have this feeling about it' (ibid.). So even if a building's full complexity may only gradually affect and move us, we instantly sense the building and its features upon entering it. This relates to the second feature emphasised by Zumthor, namely that encounters with buildings are very much bodily. We innately sense buildings, feel their material-haptic qualities, hear their sounds, see their lights, sense their temperature and smells, etc. Zumthor is at pains not only to address these sensory aspects analytically but also, and importantly, to use them in his practical work when trying to generate particular atmospheres (2006: 21).

Interestingly, Zumthor's conception of atmospheres is not confined to the interior of a building. That is, architectural atmospheres are not just about bodily engagement with the building itself. They also refer to how the building relates to its environment, or rather to how it '*becomes part of* its surroundings' (ibid. 63, italics added). Consequently, if a building does not attempt to immerse itself in its environment, it fails miserably from an atmospheric point of view. Unfortunately, this is a widespread problem with much contemporary architecture, which appears to be driven more by sheer profit or a will to build for the sake of building than by a concern with how particular buildings become constructive parts of their surroundings.

Two final comments on Zumthor are warranted here. Firstly, I have thus far focused on him because he is widely recognised for his atmospheric approach to architecture. However, other significant contemporary architects also follow this path. For example, the Japanese architects Kazuyo Sejima and Ryue Nishizawa, and their office, SANAA, produce architecture that attends to immersion, as well as to the multisensory qualities of physical design. Similarly, the Italian architect Renzo Piano once noted that before embarking on an assignment, he would visit the site of the future building and breathe in its air. A parallel gesture has been emphasised by the French architect Jean Nouvel in his *Louisiana Manifesto,* in which he underscores the importance of architecture that takes seriously the particular spirit of the place (Nouvel 2008). Of course, such atmospheric gestures are not new. As intimated above, to some extent they mark a *return* to a previous interest in atmospheric dimensions. Most notably, perhaps, the testimonies of Nouvel and Piano are emblematic of a concern with *genius loci,* i.e. the spirit of place, a notion reinvigorated by Christian Norberg-Schulz's book *Genius Loci: Towards a Phenomenology of Architecture* (1980). In it, Norberg-Schulz made a plea for foregrounding the particular spirit of place in the understanding of architecture, and linked this to an existential argument for the spatial basis of meaning and identity.

Atmospheric architecture. The 2011 Serpentine Gallery Pavilion, designed by Peter Zumthor, Serpentine Gallery, London, England.

Atmospheres of contemporary ruins. Jeanne Fredac, *Willy Flechsig,* 2011, Berlin.

Secondly, although Zumthor must be credited for capturing a series of elements that belong to the atmospheric realm, his reflections on the topic are subject to certain limitations. One is that, perhaps because his observations on architecture are so intimately tied to his practical work, Zumthor has little to offer in terms of *theorising* architectural atmospheres. Given the fact that the notion of 'atmospheres' is exceptionally slippery, considerable conceptual work is needed to pin it down. On a related note, architectural atmospheres are disconnected from broader societal issues in Zumthor's reflections. For example, attention to power and politics is entirely absent from his writings on atmospheres, despite the fact that the kinds of atmospheres he tries to create as an architect could easily be adopted by and tied to instrumental objectives, such as the search for profit or the mobilisation of political support. This book aims to take some steps towards remedying these deficiencies: it seeks to offer theoretical reflections on how to understand architectural atmospheres *and* to embed such discussions in extant social theory, as well as in broader discussions of art, capitalism, and politics.

The book is an outcome of the conference Atmospheres, Architecture and Urban Space: New Conceptions of Management and the Social, which was organised at the Copenhagen Business School, Denmark, in 2011. The keynote speakers, Gernot Böhme, Olafur Eliasson, and Juhani Pallasmaa, were invited because of their important thoughts on and/or practical contributions to the field of architecture. The aim of the conference was similar to that of this book, i.e. to provide further nourishment for recent debates on and moves towards atmospheres in both social theory and the architectural profession. Parts of the book retain the original format of conference talks.

The book opens with Juhani Pallasmaa's essay 'Space, Place, and Atmosphere: Peripheral Perception in Existential Experience', which, as the title suggests, focuses on the analysis of atmospheres from an existential and experiential point of view. In a sense, Pallasmaa is preoccupied with the same question as Zumthor: what is architectural quality? His answer can be said to be similar to Zumthor's, too: quality in architecture is about atmosphere, namely when the ambience of a space 'fuses and heightens the sensory experience'. Drawing on philosophical and neurological resources, Pallasmaa makes two important points about the experience of atmospheres. One is that atmospheres are experienced emotionally before they are understood intellectually. In other words, we sense a space and are affected by it before we arrive at an intellectual appreciation or understanding of it. This relates to Pallasmaa's second important point, namely that our pre-intellectual encounter with architecture is a multisensory experience. A space is seen, felt, heard, etc. before it is consciously and intellectually reflected upon. Interestingly – and here, in particular, he goes beyond Zumthor – Pallasmaa relates these two points to a diagnostic and a normative observation. On a diagnostic note, Pallasmaa suggests that the emphasis on vision and image in much contemporary architecture produces, as a counter-reaction, a veritable 'quest for a haptic architecture'. Here, a central difference between two types of architecture emerges: 'The architecture of the eye detaches and controls, whereas haptic and atmospheric architecture engages and unites.' Against that backdrop, Pallasmaa reaches his normative point when concluding that architects should focus less on the visual properties of their work, especially in relation to how their designs are rendered visually; instead, they should pay much closer attention to the multisensory gesture informing an atmospheric approach. In Pallasmaa's terms, such a move would amount to replacing perspectival perception with peripheral.

Pallasmaa's essay is followed by Gernot Böhme's 'Urban Atmospheres: Charting New Directions for Architecture and Urban Planning'. As the title makes plain, in this essay Böhme is preoccupied with analysing atmospheres on an urban level. While this entails situating the discussion in a somewhat different context than Pallasmaa, several key points reverberate between the two texts. For example, Böhme too emphasises that a multisensory register is needed to understand atmospheres; vision alone is insufficient to address how bodies sense spaces and their atmospheres. Relatedly, Böhme argues that an image of a city does not correspond to, nor is it able to encapsulate, its atmospheres. Again, to grasp the atmosphere of a city requires a multisensory engagement with that city, and specifically with how urban life is played out in it.

Böhme outlines different general aspects of atmospheres before moving to the urban domain. For instance, he describes how atmospheres emanate from things and persons; that we can experience such atmospheres as quasi-objective phenomena; and that the experience is nevertheless always bound to particular individuals, meaning that '[a]tmospheres are in fact characteristic manifestations of the co-presence of subject and object'. Against this backdrop, Böhme makes two central observations. Firstly, atmospheres can be produced, i.e. objects (including buildings) can be staged strategically or instrumentally in ways that affect how people experience a city – for example, the use of city lighting in the name of crime prevention. Secondly, atmospheres emerge as a result of the daily urban life of the inhabitants. That is, particular life forms give rise to particular urban atmospheres. Böhme illustrates both of these points through reference to the acoustic life of cities. However, he also goes a step further by adding, as per Pallasmaa, a more normative suggestion: that urban planning would benefit immensely from adopting an explicitly atmospheric approach. By doing so, urban planning would be better suited to grasp how purposeful attempts at generating atmospheres must relate to extant life forms. Further, urban planners would realise that, perhaps, forbearance might often be a preferred strategy.

Böhme emphasises the need for an atmospheric approach to urban planning when he – again, similar to Pallasmaa – suggests that there is also an existential issue at stake when discussing atmospheres. In Böhme's words, 'the atmosphere of an organically developed city is [...] of major importance for the inhabitants' sense of feeling sheltered and at home.' The idea that atmospheres can be approached in a manner that stresses their contribution to a sense of being at home and feeling secure is central to Christian Borch's essay, 'The Politics of Atmospheres: Architecture, Power, and the Senses'. Borch examines how recent social theory has addressed the notion of atmospheres, and here the work of Peter Sloterdijk is attributed key importance. Sloterdijk has developed a comprehensive theory of spheres, i.e. spatial configurations that provide meaning and immunity to the people who gather under them. Interestingly, Sloterdijk links this essentially existential notion not only to the field of architecture (such as how physical design amounts to sphere production), but also to analyses of atmospheric politics, i.e. the attempts to mould atmospheres – both physical and psycho-social – in order to achieve specific

Atmospheres of the modern city. Eugène Atget, *Maison Place du Caire 2* (Building, Place du Caire), 1903. Albumen silver print. 22.1 × 17.8 cm. The J. Paul Getty Museum, Los Angeles.

political objectives. Here, Borch argues, some important connections materialise between Sloterdijk's work and observations made by Böhme and Pallasmaa. Specifically, an interest in the politics of atmospheres is tied to a concern with sensory politics, i.e. the ways in which atmospheres are designed in a multisensory fashion in order to govern or induce particular behaviours. Further, such multisensory design should attract critical attention because the moulding of behaviour through, say, olfactory manipulation, mostly takes place at a non-conscious level. Consequently, the essay suggests, the design of architectural atmospheres amounts to a subtle form of power, in which people's behaviour, desires, and experiences are managed without them being consciously aware of it.

The final contribution to this book, entitled 'Atmospheres, Art, Architecture', takes the form of a conversation between Olafur Eliasson and the authors of the three essays presented above. Eliasson is widely recognised as one of the world's leading contemporary artists, and his work is renowned not least for its highly atmospheric features and attentiveness. The conversation focuses on the notion of atmospheres; on how the production of atmospheres relates to temporality; on the links between atmospheres, ecology, and contemporary capitalist production; and on some of the political implications of the atmospheric perspective. In addressing these issues, the conversation combines reflections on atmospheres, art, and architecture.

It goes without saying that the discussions of architectural atmospheres, how they are experienced, and the kinds of politics to which they give rise are far from exhausted by this book. Nevertheless, it is our hope that the book will further advance the recent social theory debates on atmospheres, as well as the growing acknowledgement of an atmospheric approach within architecture. As mentioned above, an atmospheric approach offers an important answer to the question of what constitutes architectural quality – one that extends far beyond form and function. Adopting an atmospheric perspective implies paying attention to how architecture and urban planning are able to provide nourishment to the multisensory experiences. It means acknowledging that buildings should not be conceived of as singular entities, but rather as parts of a larger atmospheric whole. Yet the atmospheric perspective also entails a keen focus on how the production of multisensory experiences can easily be **Introduction:** endowed with, or adopted by, political (or capitalist) objectives that, given **Why Atmospheres?** their multisensory nature, are not necessarily consciously recognised by people. As a result, the interest in atmospheres also amounts to a preoccupation with how power is intimately tied to atmospheric design.

As a final note, I would like to express my gratitude to the Dreyer Foundation, whose kind financial support made both the 2011 conference and this book possible.

References

Norberg-Schulz, Christian. 1980. *Genius Loci: Towards a Phenomenology of Architecture.* New York: Rizzoli.

Nouvel, Jean. 2008. *Louisiana Manifesto.* Copenhagen: Louisiana Museum of Modern Art.

Zumthor, Peter. 2006. *Atmospheres: Architectural Environments – Surrounding Objects.* Basel, Boston, and Berlin: Birkhäuser Verlag.

Industrial atmospheres. Jeanne Fredac, *General Motors, Detroit,* 2008.

Juhani Pallasmaa

Space, Place, and Atmosphere: Peripheral Perception in Existential Experience

I was very surprised indeed to learn the subject matter that I am to address here, namely 'atmospheres'. Atmosphere, ambience, and mood are rarely discussed among architects or in schools of architecture, as architectural theorising, education, and criticism tend to focus on space, form, structure, scale, detail, and light. Only during the past two decades has an experiential view begun to replace the formal understanding of this art form. Therefore, that the explicit interest in the mood of settings has arisen in a business school is unexpected – and even visionary. This conference also confirms my assumption that there are fields in production and business that are ahead of architects in the understanding of human nature and behaviour.

I am personally grateful for this opportunity, as it has obliged me to think about the role and significance of atmosphere in architecture, which I might not have done otherwise.

Fusion of the World and the Mind The character of a space or place is not merely a visual quality, as is usually assumed. The judgement of environmental character is a complex fusion of countless factors that are immediately and synthetically grasped as an overall atmosphere, feeling, mood, or ambience. 'I enter a building, see a room, and – in a fraction of a second – have this feeling about it,' confesses Peter Zumthor, one of the architects to have acknowledged the importance of architectural atmospheres (Zumthor 2006: 13). This experience is multisensory in its very essence, but it also involves judgements beyond the five Aristotelian senses, such as the senses of orientation, gravity, balance, stability, motion, duration, continuity, scale, and illumination. Indeed, the immediate judgement of the character of space calls upon our entire embodied and existential sense, and it is perceived in a diffuse and peripheral manner, rather than through precise and conscious observation. Moreover, this complex assessment projects a temporal process, as it fuses perception, memory, and imagination. Each space and place is an invitation to and a suggestion of distinct acts and activities. Atmosphere stimulates activities and guides the imagination.

In addition to environmental atmospheres, there are interpersonal atmospheres – cultural, social, family, workplace, etc. We can, perhaps, even speak of specific atmospheres on the scale of cultural or national entities. *Genius loci,* 'the spirit of place', is a similarly ephemeral, unfocused, and non-material experiential character closely related to atmosphere; we could well speak of the atmosphere of a place, which gives it its unique perceptual and memorable character and identity. Even the imagery of a painting is integrated by an overall atmosphere or feeling – the most important unifying factor in a painting is usually its specific feel for illumination and colour. Of the various art forms, music is particularly atmospheric – it has a forceful impact on our emotions and moods, regardless of how little or how much we understand musical structures intellectually. That seems to be the very reason why music plays such an important role in cinema, and why Muzak is commonly used to create atmospheric moods in public spaces, shopping malls, and even elevators. Music creates lived and existential atmospheric interior spaces, ephemeral and dynamic experiential fields, rather than distant and imposing external shapes and objects. Atmosphere emphasises a sustained being in a situation, rather than a singular moment of perception; atmosphere is always a continuum. The fact that music can move us to tears is a convincing proof of the emotive power of art, as well as of our innate capacity to internalise abstract emotive structures – or more precisely, to project our emotions onto abstractly symbolic structures. The recent discovery of 'mirror neurons', which make us unconsciously mimic others or even experience their physical sensations, suggests the quality in our neural system that makes such mimetic and emotive mirroring possible.

As we enter a space, the space enters us, and the experience is essentially an exchange and fusion of the object and the subject. Robert Pogue Harrison, an American literary scholar, states poetically: 'In the fusion of place and soul, the soul is as much of a container of place as place is a container of soul, both are susceptible to the same forces of destruction' (Harrison 2008: 130). Similarly, atmosphere is an exchange between the material or existent properties of the place and our immaterial realm of projection and imagination.

Permit me already at this early stage to suggest a definition for experiential atmosphere: Atmosphere is the overarching perceptual, sensory, and emotive impression of a space, setting, or social situation.

It provides the unifying coherence and character for a room, space, place, and landscape, or a social encounter. It is 'the common denominator', 'the colouring' or 'the feel' of the experiential situation. Atmosphere is a mental 'thing', an experiential property or characteristic that is suspended between the object and the subject.

Paradoxically, we grasp the atmosphere of a place before we identify its details or understand it intellectually. In fact, we may be completely unable to say anything meaningful about the characteristics of a situation, yet have a firm image and recall of it, as well as an emotive attitude towards it. In the same way, although we do not consciously analyse or understand the interaction of meteorological facts, we grasp the essence of weather at a glance, and it inevitably conditions our mood and intentionality. Similarly, as we enter a new city, we grasp its overall character without having consciously analysed a single one of its myriad properties. This is an intuitive and emotive capacity that seems to be biologically derived and largely unconsciously and instinctively determined through evolutionary programming. 'We perceive atmospheres through our emotional sensibility – a form of perception that works incredibly quickly, and which we humans evidently need to help us survive', Zumthor suggests (2006: 13). The new sciences of bio-psychology and ecological psychology actually study such evolutionary causalities in human behaviour and cognition (see, for instance, Hildebrand 1992; 1999). It is quite certain that we are genetically and culturally conditioned to seek or avoid certain types of atmospheres. Our shared pleasure in being in the shadow of large trees with the possibility of looking into a sunlit open field, for instance, is explained on the basis of such evolutionary programming (Wilson 1984).

Although atmosphere and mood are overarching qualities of our environments and spaces, these qualities have not been much observed, analysed, or theorised in architecture. Gernot Böhme (1995; 2006) is one of the pioneering thinkers in the philosophy of atmospheres, along with Herman Schmitz (1969). In the architectural profession, Peter Zumthor, for one, points out the significance of architectural atmospheres in his book *Atmospheres*.

Atmosphere seems to be a more conscious objective in literary, cinematic, theatrical, musical, and painterly thinking than in architecture. In fact, there is an entire painterly approach, as exemplified by J. M. W. Turner and Claude Monet, which can be called 'atmospheric painting', in the two meanings of the notion. 'Atmosphere is my style', Turner confessed to John Ruskin, as Zumthor reminds us (2006: title page). The formal and structural ingredients in the work of these artists are deliberately suppressed for the benefit of an embracing and shapeless atmosphere, suggestive of temperature, moisture, and subtle movements of the air. Similarly, 'colour field' painters suppress form and boundaries in favour of intense interaction of colour. Great films, such as those by Jean Vigo, Jean Renoir, Michelangelo Antonioni, and Andrei Tarkovsky, are also steeped in their characteristic atmospheric dramaturgy and continuum. Film music frequently plays a significant role in creating the desired ambience of romance, nostalgia, yearning, fear, or outright terror. Also, theatre relies heavily on an atmosphere that supports the integrity and continuity of the story, regardless of the often abstracted and vaguely hinted features of the place or space. The ambience can be so suggestive and dominating that very few cues of the setting are needed, as in Lars von Trier's *Dogville,* in which houses and rooms are often indicated by mere white chalk lines on a dark floor. Nonetheless, the drama takes a full grip of the spectator's imagination and emotions, and projects a fully credible and convincing atmosphere of the fictitious reality.

Somewhat paradoxically, we can also speak of 'atmospheric sculpture', such as some of the sketch-like modelled works of Medardo Rosso, Auguste Rodin, and Alberto Giacometti. The rough modelling and materiality suggest virtual movement and a carnal realism. Also, interior decorators, set designers, and commercial designers of shop interiors and exhibits, not to mention funeral parlours and wedding venues, seem to be more aware of the seminal role of ambience than architects, who tend to think more in terms of the 'pure' qualities of space, form, and geometry. Among architects, atmosphere is judged as something romantic and shallowly entertaining. The serious Western tradition is entirely based on seeing architecture as a material and geometric object through focused vision, whereas ambience is a kind of an immaterial 'halo' that the material reality

Art and architecture articulate our existential experiences; artistic works enable us to sense 'how the world touches us', as Maurice Merleau-Ponty describes the impact of the paintings of Paul Cézanne. | Sigurdur Gudmundsson, *Collage, 1979,* photo, text, 85 × 91 cm.

Juhani Pallasmaa

Space, Place,
and Atmosphere:
Peripheral
Perception
in Existential
Experience

seems to extrude. Ambience is like an invisible fragrance or smell that fuses and heightens the sensory experience. Besides, architectural images are usually expected to seek clarity rather than ephemerality and obscurity, a finiteness rather than open-endedness and deliberate vagueness.

Recognition of Place and Space The instant recognition of the inherent nature of a place is akin to the animalistic, automatic reading of identities and essences in the biological world. Animals possess an instant recognition of other creatures crucial to their survival – be they prey or predator. We humans identify individual faces among thousands of almost identical facial configurations, and recognise the emotive meaning of each one on the basis of minute muscular expressions. A landscape, space, or a place is an image, a mental or neural 'creature', a singular experience, that is fused with our very existential experience and cognition. Once we have assessed a space as inviting and pleasant, or uninviting and depressing, it is difficult to alter that first-hand judgement. We become attached to certain settings and remain alienated in others, and both intuitive choices are equally difficult to verbally analyse or alter as experiential realities.

Sir Colin St John Wilson explains this irresistible force of architecture and physical settings: 'It is as if I am being manipulated by some subliminal code, not to be translated into words, which acts directly on the nervous system and imagination, at the same time stirring intimations of meaning with vivid spatial experience as though they were one thing. It is my belief that the code acts so directly and vividly upon us because it is strangely familiar; it is in fact the first language we ever learned, long before words, and which is now recalled to us through art, which alone holds the key to revive it' (1979).

When describing his creative process in the essay 'The Trout and the Mountain Stream', Alvar Aalto confesses: 'Led by my instincts I draw, not architectural syntheses, but sometimes even childish compositions, and via this route I eventually arrive at an abstract basis to the main concept, a kind of universal substance with whose help the numerous quarrelling sub-problems [of the design task] can be brought into harmony' (1978: 97).

Embracing atmospheric painting: 'Atmosphere is my style', Turner once confessed to John Ruskin. | William Turner, *Rain, Steam, and Speed – The Great Western Railway*, 1844. Oil on canvas, 91 × 121.8 cm. National Gallery London.

Aalto's notion of 'universal substance' seems to refer to a unifying atmosphere or intuitive feeling rather than any conceptual, intellectual, or formal idea.

The existential value of a diffuse but comprehensive grasp of the ambience of a spatial entity, or of an entire landscape, is rather easy to understand from the point of view of the biological principle of survival. It evidently constitutes an evolutionary advantage to be instantly able to differentiate a scene of potential danger from a setting of safety and nourishment. Let me repeat, such judgements cannot be consciously deduced from details; they have to be instantaneously grasped as an intuitive reading based on a 'polyphonic' grasp of the ambience. In fact, research has established that the first wave of perceptual information is directed to the deeper, more primordial and deeply biologically conditioned parts of our neural system. This polyphonic perception and cognition has also been identified as one of the conditions for the creative mind.

At this point, I wish to suggest that the elementarist idea of perception, imagery, and thought is questionable, if not altogether wrong. An elementarist approach to architecture and architectural education is equally misguided.

Unconscious Perception and Creative Thought I recently penned a psychoanalytic study of creative imagery – or rather, of perception and imagery in the creative process – with the title 'In Praise of Vagueness: Diffuse Perception and Uncertain Thought'. Without going further into the subject matter of my essay in this context, I merely wish to say that, against the common understanding, creativity is also based on vague, polyphonic, and mostly unconscious modes of perception and thought instead of focused and unambiguous attention. Similarly, unconscious and unfocused creative scanning enables complex entities and processes to be grasped without consciously understanding any of the elements – much in the way that we grasp the entities of atmospheres. Even infants grasp the meanings of complex situations 'syncretically', without understanding separate details.

I am referring to these studies and theories of the creative mind only to underline the little-known fact that we have unexpected synthesising capacities of which we are not usually aware, and which we do not tend to regard as areas of special intelligence and value. The biased focus on rational logic and its value in human mental life is a major reason behind this unfortunate rejection. Indeed, it is surprising that more than a century after Sigmund Freud's revolutionary discoveries, the prevailing pedagogic philosophies and practices continue to grossly undervalue the entire universe of unconscious and embodied processes. Architectural education, too, continues to emphasise focused attention and conscious intentionality.

We have traditionally underestimated the roles and cognitive capacities of emotions in comparison with our conceptual, intellectual, and verbal understanding. Yet emotional reactions are often the most comprehensive and synthetic judgements that we can produce, although we are hardly able to identify the constituents of these assessments. When we fear or love something, there is little scope or need for rationalisation.

In addition, our accepted understanding of intelligence is grossly limited. Recent psychological studies have revealed seven or ten different categories of intelligence beyond the narrow realm of intelligence measured by the standard IQ test. The American psychologist Howard Gardner lists seven categories of intelligence: linguistic intelligence; logical-mathematical intelligence; musical intelligence; bodily-kinaesthetic intelligence; spatial intelligence; interpersonal intelligence; and intrapersonal intelligence (Gardner 1999: 41–43). Later in his book, he suggests three further categories: naturalistic intelligence; spiritual intelligence; and existential intelligence (1999: 47). I would definitely add the categories of emotional, aesthetic, and ethical intelligence to this list of human cognitive capacities – and I would even suggest atmospheric intelligence as a specific and significant realm of human intelligence.

Space and Imagination Our innate capacity to grasp comprehensive atmospheres and moods is akin to our capacity to project imaginatively the emotively suggestive settings of an entire novel as we read it. We live simultaneously in material and mental worlds that are constantly fused. When reading a great novel, we constantly construct the settings and situations of the story at the suggestion of the author's words. We

Atmospheric contemporary art that simulates the effect of weather. Olafur Eliasson, *The weather project*. The Turbine Hall, Tate Modern, London.

move effortlessly and seamlessly from one setting to the next, as if they pre-existed as physical realities prior to our act of reading. Indeed, as we move from one scene to the next, the settings seem to be there ready for us to enter. Remarkably, we do not experience these imaginary spaces as pictures, but in their full spatiality and atmosphere. The same fullness applies to our dreams – dreams are not pictures, they are spaces and imaginatively lived experiences. Yet they are all entirely products of our imagination.

The processes of literary imagination are discussed in Elaine Scarry's recent book *Dreaming by the Book.* She explains the vividness of a profound literary text as follows: 'In order to achieve the "vivacity" of the material world, the verbal arts must somehow also imitate its "persistence" and, most crucially, its quality of "givenness". It seems almost certainly the case that it is the "instructional" character of the verbal arts that fulfils this mimetic requirement for "givenness"' (2001: 30).

Bohumil Hrabal, the Czech writer, points out the concreteness of our literary imagination: 'When I read, I don't really read: I pop up a beautiful sentence in my mouth and suck it like liqueur until the thought dissolves in me like alcohol, infusing my brain and heart and coursing on through the veins to the root of each blood vessel' (1990: 1).

Architecture, too, calls for a deepened sense of materiality, gravity, and reality, not an air of entertainment or fantasy. Besides, architecture requires an integrating and emotively suggestive atmosphere. As Constantin Brancusi requests: 'Art must give suddenly, all at once, the shock of life, the sensation of breathing' (Brancusi, quoted in Shanes 1989: 67). The power of architecture lies in its ability to strengthen the experience of the real, and its imaginative dimension arises from this strengthened and re-sensitised sense of reality, an experience of 'thick' space and time.

Experiencing, memorising, and imagining spatial settings, situations, and events engages our imaginative skills. Even the acts of experiencing and memorising are embodied acts, in which lived embodied imagery evokes an imaginative reality that feels similar to actual experience. Recent studies have revealed that the acts of perception and imagining take place in the same areas of the brain and, consequently, these acts are closely related (Kojo 1996). Even perception calls for imagination, as percepts are not automatic products of our sensory mechanisms; they are essentially creations and products of intentionality and imagination. Arthur Zajonc argues that we could not even see light without our mental 'inner light' (Zajonc 1995).

The most amazing feature of our mental acts is the synthetic completeness of the imagery. As we read a great novel, we create the urban or landscape settings as well as the buildings, spaces and rooms and feel their ambience – albeit without being able to focus on any of their details. Undoubtedly, the totality dominates the detail and this principle actually reflects the way our mind works.

Atmosphere or ambience is an epic experiential dimension or prediction, as we automatically read behavioural and social aspects – existent, potential, or imaginary – into the atmospheric image. We also read a temporal layering or narrative into the setting, and we have an emotional appreciation of the layering of temporal cues and traces, as well as images of past life in our settings. We like to be connected with signs of life instead of being isolated in hermetic and artificial conditions. Don't we seek historically dense settings because they connect us experientially and imaginatively with past life, and because it makes us feel safe and enriched to be part of that temporal continuum? Traces of life support images of safety and generate images of continued life.

We do not judge environments merely by our senses, we also test and evaluate them through our sense of imagination. Comforting and inviting settings inspire our unconscious imagery, daydreams, and fantasy. As Gaston Bachelard argues: '[T]he chief benefit of the house [is that] the house shelters daydreaming, the house protects the dreamer, the house allows one to dream in peace [...] [T]he house is one of the greatest powers of integration for the thoughts, memories, and dreams of mankind' (1969: 6).

Herbert Marcuse, the social psychologist, also acknowledges the connection between the atmospheres of settings and our fantasies, as he makes the thought-provoking suggestion that the alarming increase of sexual violence and distorted sexuality today is a consequence of the fact that our modern settings do not stimulate and support erotic fantasies.[1]

Atmospheric architecture: the living space of the Villa Mairea is a haptic fusion of tectonic architectural space and an amorphous and spontaneously rhythmic 'forest space'. | Alvar Aalto, Villa Mairea, Noormarkku, Finland, 1938–9.

The atmosphere of contemporary cityscapes and dwellings frequently lacks a stimulating, sensuous, and erotic air.

'Understanding' the Artistic Image We have been taught to conceive, observe, and evaluate architectural spaces and settings primarily as aesthetic and visual entities. Yet, the diffuse overall ambience is often much more decisive and powerful in determining our attitude to the setting. Often, buildings and details that hardly possess any aesthetic values manage to create a sensorially rich and pleasant atmosphere. Vernacular settings and traditional towns are examples of pleasant atmospheres often arising from rather uninteresting units. Such atmospheres are most often created by a specific materiality, scale, rhythm, colour, or formal theme with variations. In architectural education, we are usually advised to develop our designs from elementary aspects towards larger entities, but our perceptions and experiential judgements seem to advance in the reverse manner – from the entity down to details. When experiencing a work of art, the whole gives meaning to the parts, not the other way round. We need to grasp complete images instead of elements, and, in fact, there are no 'elements' in the world of artistic expression; there are only complete poetic images intertwined with distinct emotive orientations. Every profound work of art is a microcosm.

Works of art mentally and emotionally affect us long before we understand them. Indeed, we usually do not 'understand' the works at all. I would venture to argue that the greater the artistic work, the less we understand it intellectually. A distinct mental short-circuiting between the lived and emotive encounter and intellectual 'understanding' is a constitutive character of the artistic image. This is also the view of Semir Zeki, one of today's leading neurologists. He regards a high degree of ambiguity, such as the unfinished imagery of Michelangelo's slaves or the ambivalent human narratives of Vermeer's paintings, as essential contributors to the greatness of these works (Zeki 1999: 22–36). In reference to the great capacity of profound artists to evoke, manipulate, and direct our emotions, Zeki makes the surprising argument: 'Most painters are also neurologists' (1999: 2).

Highly atmospheric architectural minimalism that creates a strong, embracing, and tactile feeling through a rigorous use of geometry, materials, and light. | Peter Zumthor, Thermal Baths Vals, Graubünden, 1996.

Multisensory Experience: The Significance of Touch Every signifi- cant experience of architecture is multisensory; qualities of matter, space, and scale are measured by the eye, ear, nose, skin, tongue, skeleton, and muscle. Ultimately, we sense works of art and architecture through our senses of self and existence. Maurice Merleau-Ponty emphasises this simultaneity of experience and sensory interaction: 'My perception is [therefore] not a sum of visual, tactile, and audible givens: I perceive in a total way with my whole being: I grasp a unique structure of the thing, a unique way of being, which speaks to all my senses at once' (1964: 48).

Even the eye collaborates with the other senses. All of the senses, including vision, are extensions of the sense of touch: the senses are specialisations of the skin, and all sensory experiences are related to tactility. We can also acknowledge that overpowering atmospheres have a haptic, almost material presence, as if we were surrounded and embraced by a specific substance. The anthropologist Ashley Montagu confirms the primacy of the tactile realm based on medical evidence: '[The skin] is the oldest and the most sensitive of our organs, our first medium of communication, and our most efficient protector [...] Even the transparent cornea of the eye is overlain by a layer of modified skin [...] Touch is the parent of our eyes, ears, nose, and mouth. It is the sense that became differentiated into the others, a fact that seems to be recognised in the age-old evaluation of touch as "the mother of the senses"' (1971: 3).

Touch is the sensory mode that integrates our experiences of the world and of ourselves. Even visual perceptions are united and integrated into the haptic continuum of the sense of self; my body remembers who I am and where I am placed in the world. In the opening chapter of *Combray,* Marcel Proust describes how the protagonist wakes up in his bed and gradually reconstructs his world on the basis of his body memory: 'the composite memory of its [his body's] ribs, its knees, its shoulder-blades' (1996: 4).

The retinally biased architecture of our time is clearly giving rise to a quest for a haptic architecture. Montagu sees a wider change taking place in Western consciousness: 'We in the Western world are beginning to discover our neglected senses. This growing awareness represents something of an overdue insurgency against the painful deprivation of sensory experience we have suffered in our technologised world' (1971: XIII). Our culture of control and speed has favoured the architecture of the eye, with its instantaneous imagery and distanced impact, whereas haptic and atmospheric architecture promotes slowness and intimacy, appreciated and comprehended gradually as images of the body and the skin. The architecture of the eye detaches and controls, whereas haptic and atmospheric architecture engages and unites. Tactile sensibility replaces distancing visual imagery through enhanced materiality, nearness, identification, and intimacy.

Material Imagination The atmosphere of a setting is often generated by a strong presence of materiality. The heightened experience of materiality strengthens the feeling of reality and temporality. But the dominant atmospheric feature of a place may well be an acoustical character, a smell, or even especially pleasant or unpleasant weather.

In his phenomenological investigation of poetic imagery, Gaston Bachelard makes a distinction between 'formal imagination' and 'material imagination' (1983: 1). He suggests that images arising from matter project deeper and more profound experiences than images arising from form. Matter evokes unconscious images and emotions, but modernity at large has been primarily concerned with form. However, an engagement with the material imagination seems to characterise the entire 'other tradition of modernism', to use the title of Colin St John Wilson's book (1995). Accordingly, this architecture, such as the works of Sigurd Lewerentz, Hans Scharoun, Gunnar Asplund and Alvar Aalto, is also highly atmospheric.

Ruination, destruction, weathering, and wear strengthen the atmospheric impact of architecture (Leatherbarrow and Mostafavi 1993). In an essay on the theatre director Peter Brook's destructive manipulation of the architectural space of the Théâtre des Bouffes du Nord in Paris for theatrical purposes, Andrew Todd writes: 'The walls engage time in a complex way. There is an after-echo of the original bourgeois music hall form, and this is rendered profound, even tragic, by the opening up of the layers of time on the walls. The top skin, which seals the imagination at a specific style or period, has been scorched away, so the walls exist in an indeterminate time, partway between cultural definition and eschatological

Architectural minimalism aiming at the sensitisation of the senses, particularly that of hearing. The surface textures and colours aim at activating peripheral vision prior to the musical performance. | Juhani Pallasmaa, Korundi Art Center, Rovaniemi, Lapland, 2012. The Music Hall.

dissolution. But this is no dead ruin: Brook has not been afraid to bash the place around a little more, breaking holes, putting in doors [...] One can also speak of another virtual patina the walls have acquired through the accruing memory of Brook's work in there' (1999: 4).

In Rainer Maria Rilke's stunning chapter in *The Notebooks of Malte Laurids Brigge,* the protagonist comprehends the life that has been lived in a demolished house through the traces it has left on the end wall of the neighbouring building – in fact these are signs by which the young man reconstructs essential aspects of his own childhood and self (Rilke 1992).

A similar atmospheric 'weakening' of formal architectural logic takes place in the reuse and renovation of buildings. The insertion of new functional, aesthetic, and symbolic structures short-circuits the initial architectural logic of the building and opens up unexpected emotional and expressive ranges of experience. Architectural settings that layer contradictory ingredients project a special sensory richness and empathetic charm. Often, the most enjoyable museum, office, or residential space is that which has been installed in an adapted existing building.

The ecological approach also favours an adaptive image, parallel to the inherent 'weakness' of ecologically adapted processes. This ecological fragility is reflected in contemporary art – for instance, in the poetic works of Richard Long, Hamish Fulton, Wolfgang Leib, Andy Goldsworthy, and Nils-Udo, all of which are engaged in a subtle dialogue with nature. Here again, artists set an example for architects.

Gardening is an art form inherently engaged with time, change, atmosphere, and fragile image. On the other hand, the geometric garden exemplifies the traditional Western attempt to domesticate nature into patterns of man-made geometry. The tradition of landscape and garden architecture provides inspiration for an architecture liberated from the constraints of geometric and strong image. Biological models have already entered various fields of science, medicine, and engineering; the use of biological models for human innovations is nowadays often called 'bio-mimicry' (see Benuys 1997). Why should biological models not be valid in architecture? Indeed, the more subtle line of high-tech architecture is already heading in that direction.

Perspectival Space and Peripheral Vision The all-encompassing and instantaneous perception of atmospheres calls for a specific manner of perception – unconscious and unfocused peripheral perception. This fragmented percept of the world is actually our normal reality, although we believe that we perceive everything with precision. Our image of the world is held together by constant active scanning by the senses, movement, and a creative fusion and interpretation of our inherently fragmented percepts.

The historical development of the representational techniques depicting space and form is closely tied to the development of architecture itself. The perspectival understanding of space gave rise to an architecture of vision, whereas the quest to liberate the eye from its perspectival fixation has enabled the conception of multi-perspectival, simultaneous, and atmospheric space. Perspectival space leaves us as outside observers, whereas multi-perspectival and atmospheric space and peripheral vision encloses and enfolds us in its embrace. This is the perceptual and psychological essence of Impressionist, Cubist, and Abstract Expressionist space – we are pulled into the space and made to experience it as a fully embodied sensation and a thick atmosphere. The special reality of a Cézanne landscape or Jackson Pollock painting, as well as of engaging architecture and cityscapes, derives from the way these experiential situations engage our perceptual and psychological mechanisms.

While the hectic eye of the camera captures a momentary situation, a passing condition of light or an isolated, framed, and focused fragment, the real experience of architectural reality depends fundamentally on peripheral and anticipated vision; the mere experience of interiority implies peripheral perception. The perceptual realm that we sense beyond the sphere of focused vision is as important as the focused image that can be frozen by the camera. In fact, there is evidence that peripheral and unconscious perception is more important for our perceptual and mental system than focused perception.[2]

This assumption suggests that one reason why contemporary spaces often alienate us – compared with historical and natural settings, which elicit powerful emotional identification and engagement – has to do with the poverty of our peripheral vision. Focused vision makes us mere outside observers; peripheral perception transforms retinal images into a spatial and bodily involvement and gives rise to the sense of atmosphere and participation. Peripheral perception is the perceptival mode through which we grasp atmospheres. The importance of the senses of hearing, smell, and touch (temperature, moisture, air movement) for atmospheric perception arises from their essence as non-directional senses and their embracing character. The role of peripheral and unconscious perception explains why a photographic image is usually an unreliable witness of true architectural quality. Indeed, architects would do better if they were less concerned with the photogenic qualities of their works.

Even creative activity calls for an unfocused and undifferentiated subconscious mode of vision, one fused with integrative tactile experience (see Ehrenzweig 1973). The object of a creative act is not only enfolded by the eye and the touch, it has to be introjected, identified with one's own body and existential experience.[3] In deep thought, focused vision is blocked and thoughts travel with an absent-minded gaze. In creative work, both the scientist and the artist directly engage with their corporeal, existential, and atmospheric experience, rather than with an external logical problem.

Today's urgent call for an ecologically sustainable architecture also suggests an non-autonomous and collaborative architecture adapted to precise conditions of topography, soil, climate, and vegetation, as well as other conditions of the region and site. The potentials of atmosphere, weak gestalt, and adaptive fragility will undoubtedly be explored in the near future, in the search for an architecture that will acknowledge the conditions and principles of ecological reality as well as of our own bio-historical nature. I suggest that in the near future we will be more interested in atmospheres than individually expressive forms. Understanding atmospheres will most likely teach us about the secret power of architecture and how it can guide large masses, but at the same time, enable us to create our own individual existential foothold with dignity.

'The richest experiences happen long before the soul takes notice. And when we begin to open our eyes to the visible, we have already been supporters of the invisible for a long time' (Gabriele d'Annunzio, as quoted in Bachelard 1983: 16).

Footnotes

1 According to Marcuse (1991: 73), 'a whole dimension of human activity and passivity has been de-eroticized. The environment from which the individual could obtain pleasure – which he could cathect as gratifying almost as an extended zone of the body – has been rigidly reduced. Consequently the "universe" of libidinous cathexis is likewise reduced. The effect is a localisation and contraction of libido, the reduction of erotic to sexual experience and satisfaction'.

2 Anton Ehrenzweig offers the medical case of hemianopia as a proof for the priority of peripheral vision in the psychic condition of our mechanism of sight. In a case of this rare illness, one half of the visual field turns blind while the other retains vision. In some cases of the illness, the field of vision later reorganises itself into a new and complete circular field of vision, with a new sharp focus at the centre, surrounded by an unfocused field. As the new focus is formed, the reorganisation implies that parts of the former peripheral field of inaccurate vision acquire visual acuity – and more significantly, the area of former focused vision gives up its capacity for sharp vision as it transforms into a part of the new unfocused peripheral field. 'These case histories prove, if proof is needed, that an overwhelming psychological need exists that requires us to have the larger part of the visual field in a vague medley of images', Ehrenzweig notes (1973: 284).

3 The word 'introjection' in psychoanalytic language refers to the manner in which children in their early life experience and internalise aspects of the world through their mouth.

References

Aalto, Alvar. 1978. 'The Trout and the Mountain Stream'. In *Sketches,* edited by Göran Schildt, 96–102. Cambridge, MA: MIT Press.

Bachelard, Gaston. 1969. *The Poetics of Space.* Boston: Beacon Press.

Bachelard, Gaston. 1983. *Water and Dreams: An Essay on the Imagination of Matter.* Dallas, TX: The Pegasus Foundation.

Benuys, Janine M. 1997. *Biomimicry.* New York: William Morrow.

Böhme, Gernot. 1995. *Atmosphäre.* Frankfurt am Main: Suhrkamp Verlag.

Böhme, Gernot. 2006. *Architektur und Atmosphäre.* Munich: Wilhelm Fink.

Ehrenzweig, Anton. 1973. *The Hidden Order of Art.* Frogmore, St. Albans: Paladin.

Gardner, Howard. 1999. *Intelligence Reframed: Multiple Intelligences for the 21st Century.* New York: Basic Books.

Harrison, Robert Pogue. 2008. *Gardens: An Essay on the Human Condition.* Chicago and London: University of Chicago Press.

Hildebrand, Grant. 1992. *The Wright Space: Pattern and Meaning in Frank Lloyd Wright's Houses.* Seattle: University of Washington Press.

Hildebrand, Grant. 1999. *The Origins of Architectural Pleasure.* Berkeley, Los Angeles: University of California Press.

Hrabal, Bohumil. 1990. *Too Loud a Solitude.* Translated by Michael Henry Heim. San Diego, New York, and London: Harcourt, Inc.

Kojo, Ilpo. 1996. 'Mielikuvat ovat aivoille todellisia' [Images are real for the brain]. *Helsingin Sanomat,* March 16.

Leatherbarrow, David, and Mohsen Mostafavi. 1993.

On Weathering: The Life of Buildings in Time. Cambridge, MA: MIT Press.

Marcuse, Herbert. 1991. *The One-Dimensional Man: Studies in the Ideology of Advanced Industrial Society.* Boston: Beacon Press.

Merleau-Ponty, Maurice. 1964. 'The Film and the New Psychology'. In *Sense and Non-Sense,* 48–59. Evanston, IL: Northwestern University Press.

Montagu, Ashley. 1971. *Touching: The Human Significance of the Skin.* New York: Harper & Row.

Pallasmaa, Juhani. 2012. 'In Praise of Vagueness: Diffuse Perception and Uncertain Thought'. In *Space & Psyche.* Edited by Elizabeth Danze and Stephen Sonneberg. Austin: Center for Architecture and Design, University of Texas.

Proust, Marcel. 1996. In *Search of Lost Time: Volume 1 – Swann's Way.* London: Vintage Books.

Rilke, Rainer Maria. 1992. *The Notebooks of Malte Laurids Brigge.* New York and London: W. W. Norton & Co.

Scarry, Elaine. 2001. *Dreaming by the Book.* Princeton, NJ: Princeton University Press.

Schmitz, Hermann. 1969. *System der Philosophie, vol. 3, Der Raum, Part 2, Der Gefühlsraum.* Bonn: Bouvier.

Shanes, Eric. 1989. *Constantin Brancusi.* New York: Abbeville Press.

Todd, Andrew. 1999. 'Learning From Peter Brook's Work on Theatre Space'. Unpublished manuscript, September 25.

Wilson, Colin St John. 1979. 'Architecture – Public Good and Private Necessity'. *RIBA Journal* 3: 107–15.

Wilson, Colin St John. 1995. *The Other Tradition of Modern Architecture.* London: Academy Editions.

Wilson, Edward O. 1984. 'The Right Place'. In *Biophilia: The Human Bond with Other Species,* 103–18. Cambridge, MA: Harvard University Press.

Zajonc, Arthur. 1995. *Catching the Light: The Entwined History of Light and Mind.* New York and Oxford: Oxford University Press.

Zeki, Semir. 1999. *Inner Vision: An Exploration of Art and the Brain.* Oxford: Oxford University Press.

Zumthor, Peter. 2006. *Atmospheres: Architectural Environments – Surrounding Objects.* Basel, Boston, and Berlin: Birkhäuser Verlag.

Gernot Böhme

**Urban Atmospheres:
Charting New
Directions for
Architecture and
Urban Planning**

Introduction

Colloquial 'Atmosphere' is a colloquial term, yet despite or perhaps because of the ambiguity of its usage, it is helpful to return to it again and again. We speak of the tense atmosphere of a meeting, the light-hearted atmosphere of a day, the gloomy atmosphere of a vault. We refer to the atmosphere of a city, a restaurant, a landscape. The notion of atmosphere always concerns a spatial sense of ambience. An extraordinarily rich vocabulary may be used to describe it: cheerful, sublime, melancholy, stuffy, oppressive, tense, uplifting. We also speak of the atmosphere of the 1920s, of a petty bourgeois atmosphere, of the atmosphere of power. The term itself, 'atmosphere', derives from meteorology and, as a designation for an ambient quality, has a number of synonyms that likewise connote the airy, cloudy, or indefinite: these include climate, nimbus, aura, fluid; and perhaps emanation should be counted among them as well.

Between As an aesthetic concept, atmosphere acquires definition through its relation to other concepts and through the aesthetic constellations it creates. Atmosphere is the prototypical 'between' phenomenon. Accordingly, it is a difficult thing to put into words given the background of European ontology – Japanese philosophers have an easier time of it with expressions such as *ki* or *aidagara.* Atmosphere is something between the subject and the object; therefore, aesthetics of atmosphere must also mediate between the aesthetics of reception and the aesthetics of the product or of production. Such aesthetics no longer maintain that artistic activity is consummated in the creation of a work and that this product is then available for reception, whether from a hermeneutical or a critical standpoint. An aesthetics of atmospheres pertains to artistic activity that consists of the production of particular receptions, or to types of reception by viewers or consumers that play a role in the production of the 'work' itself. Atmospheres fill spaces; they emanate from things, constellations of things and persons. The individual as a recipient can happen upon them, be assailed by them; we experience them, in other words, as something quasi-objective, the existence of which we can also communicate with others. Yet they cannot be defined independently from the persons emotionally affected by them; they are subjective facts (Schmitz 2007: 54–65).

River Kamo: Life alongside the rivers, 2005–7.

Atmospheres can be produced consciously through objective arrangements, light, and music – here, the art of the stage set is paradigmatic (see Böhme 2011). But what they are, their character, must always be felt – by exposing ourselves to them, we experience the impression that they make. Atmospheres are in fact characteristic manifestations of the co-presence of subject and object.

Staging The aesthetics of atmospheres is capable of addressing a broad spectrum of aesthetic work that, in traditional aesthetics, occupied a marginal place or at best was labelled 'applied art', ranging from architecture and stage design to design and advertising. This is the area in which the desired transformation of art into life was actually accomplished by the avant-garde. Today there is no area of life, not a product, installation, or collection, that is not the explicit object of design (see Böhme 2008). What was still a revolutionary act in art – the departure from the object – is here a method. For all the talk of design, things and their form are not what are at stake. Rather, the focus is on scenes, life spaces, charisma. Here, atmosphere is the explicit object and the goal of aesthetic action. The aesthetics of atmosphere directs attention to what had always taken place in these areas of aesthetic work, though an ontology oriented to the thing had distorted it. Instead, the object and goal of aesthetic work is literally nothing; i.e. that which lies 'between', the space. The architect may share facades and views with the painter, but what belongs to the architect is the shaping of space with confinement and expanse, with direction, with lightness and heaviness. To be sure, the designer also gives objects form. But what matters are their radiance, their impressions, the suggestions of motion. Naturally, in advertising, information and representation are important too – but much more so the staging of products and their presentation as ingredients of a lifestyle.

Social Atmospheres However, atmospheres result not only from the interaction of objects and non-material factors such as light and sound, but also from persons. Indeed, the talk of atmospheres is most familiar from the social context, i.e. conferences, political meetings, and face-to-face communication. Every personal communication takes place in a

Gernot Böhme

**Urban Atmospheres:
Charting New
Directions for
Architecture and
Urban Planning**

certain mood, which emanates from the physiognomy and the behaviour of the people in question. Here, everybody has a certain atmospheric competence, insofar as he or she more or less consciously contributes to the common atmosphere. This is effected, for example, through modulation of voice, but there are even certain rules according to which we can expect to produce an intended atmosphere, for example politeness. Mass psychology also speaks of atmosphere in terms of a common mood or emotion in the air, which enraptures individuals in the crowd and integrates them into the collective.

Construction and Criticism Atmospheres are experienced as an emotional effect. For this reason, the art of producing them – above all in music, but also throughout the entire spectrum of aesthetic work, from the stage set to the orchestration of mass demonstrations, from the design of malls to the imposing architecture of court buildings – is at all times also an exercise of power. In analysing how atmospheres are produced, the aesthetics of atmospheres will hardly provide instruction for practitioners; rather the reverse, aesthetics must learn from practitioners. It will, however, afford a necessary critical potential. Today, aesthetics is no longer by any account the beautification of life or the appearance of reconciliation; rather, with the aestheticisation of politics (Benjamin 1973) and the staging of everyday life (Durth 1988), it has itself become a political power and an economic factor.

The Atmosphere of a City
It is not at all unusual to speak of the 'atmosphere of a city'. We find the expression in everyday speech and in writing, in advertising material for cities and in the travel supplements of newspapers. For this use of the term in ordinary language, two things apply: first, *atmosphere* is mentioned, as a rule, from or for the perspective of the stranger; secondly, it is an attempt to identify something characteristic about a city. When we speak of atmosphere as something that is experienced by strangers to the city, this should not be taken to imply that we mean the city from the tourist's perspective. Rather, what is meant by atmosphere is that which is commonplace and self-evident for the inhabitants and which is constantly

46

Daitokuji: Buddhist temple area, 2005–7.
Entsuji-Temple: View through the Buddhist garden including the landscape: Hiei-san, 2005–7.

produced by the locals through their lives, but which is noticed first by the stranger as a characteristic. This is why the atmosphere of a city is not the same as its image. The image of a city is the consciously projected self-portrait and the sum of its advantages that an outsider might enjoy. Moreover – to come to the second point – by 'the atmosphere of a city' we understand something characteristic, that is, something peculiar to the city, what makes it individual and therefore cannot be communicated in general concepts. That does not, however, mean that we cannot talk about the atmosphere of a city – we will see that that is indeed possible. Rather, what it means is that atmosphere is something that has to be *sensed* in order to understand what is really at stake when we talk about atmosphere. The atmosphere of a city is precisely the way life goes on within it.

Working the 'lifeworldly' meaning of atmosphere into a concept in aesthetic theory (Böhme 2013) is first of all advantageous to aesthetic theory itself; in this case, to the aesthetics of the city. Introducing the concept liberates this aesthetics from being restricted to the visual and symbolic. Anything that cannot be grasped in structures is shifted to 'meanings'. Thus, for instance, there is talk of *The Meaning in Western Architecture* (Norberg-Schulz 1977) or of *The Language of Post-Modern Architecture* (Jencks 1984). Here, however, we are just following the trend set by semiotics, and we fail to realise that the age of representation has long since come to an end (Redner 1994). To put it another way, the multi-cultural world of our large cities does indeed contain more and more universally understood pictograms, but it no longer has a symbolism that is understood by the community as a whole. As a result, that which appeals to us in a city cannot be construed as language; instead, it enters our disposition through the impression it makes (in German, *Anmutungscharakter*).

This brings us to the second advantage of the concept of atmosphere for an aesthetics of the city. In such an aesthetics, it is a matter not of how a city should be judged in terms of aesthetic or cultural aspects, but of how we feel in this city. Here we are taking a decisive step towards including what has been called, somewhat inappropriately, the 'subjective factor'. Of course, we not only sense an atmosphere in our own perception, but we sense it as something that radiates from another person, from

Urban Atmospheres: Charting New Directions for Architecture and Urban Planning

Hiei-san: The holy mountain visible from almost everywhere in Kyoto, 2005–7.

things or from the surroundings. To that extent, it is something subjective that can be shared with others and about which an understanding can be reached. In studying atmospheres, it is a question of how we feel in surroundings of a particular quality – that is, how we sense these qualities in our own disposition. We can reach agreement on such dispositions by pointing out their character. An atmosphere can be relaxed or oppressive; it can be business-like, jovial, or festive. Our languages have countless expressions for characterising atmospheres, whereby we can distinguish five main groups. First, our languages have terms for synaesthetic character, that which is sensed primarily in a modification of our bodily disposition. Second, we have moods or feelings in the narrower sense, like joy, sorrow, seriousness. Third, there are so-called suggestions of movement, like pressing, elevating. Fourth, there are terms for social characters, for example, if a conversation takes place in a cold or warm atmosphere. And finally, we have atmospheres that are coined by social conventions. Examples of the latter are elegant, petty bourgeois, meagre. Using atmospheric characteristics to help analyse urban environments would be, historically speaking, an extension of what Hirschfeld (1779) introduced in his descriptions of park scenes. It would aim at determining urban environments with respect to the 'feeling of life' (*Lebensgefühl*) for those who live in them or who visit them, and would include identifying the causes of possible pathologies.

The third advantage in the concept of atmosphere is found on the objective side. We cannot study atmospheres solely from the side of the subject – that is, by exposing ourselves to them; they can also be studied from the side of the object – that is, from the side of the agencies (*Instanzen*) by means of which they are created. Stage design provides the paradigm for this perspective. The general aim of stage design is to create an atmosphere with the help of lights, music, sound, spatial constellations, and the use of characteristic objects. Yet the paradigm of stage design falls short in the case of city planning, inasmuch as the atmosphere in the latter is created not for the outside observer but for the actors, as it were – that is, for the participants in urban life, who together produce the urban atmosphere through their own activities.

Generators of Atmosphere

With regard to the domains or dimensions of the generators of atmosphere, I would like to concentrate in my examples on those that have so far enjoyed little attention in the literature on city aesthetics and city planning, or have found no place there at all. I am referring to the domains of the acoustic and of life forms. Of course, the dimension of the visual, as well as spatial structures and visible forms, incorporates generators of atmosphere, or can be interpreted in this way. Correspondingly, for instance, it is not a question of what form a building has or how a city is structured, but of what these features cause it to radiate or in what way it codetermines the dispositions of the inhabitants. Models based on such an interpretation can indeed be found in classical literature – for instance, the question of orientation is central in Kevin Lynch's (1960) writings. Similarly, Cullen occasionally speaks of the significance of the geometric structure he identifies for 'the position of our body' (1960: 9). To be more precise, here it would be a question not simply of relative positions, but of how we are bodily disposed in such and such a structured space. It does make a difference whether we go through narrow lanes or across wide esplanades; whether winding hilly streets or long straight ones are characteristic of a city; whether among the skyscrapers we suddenly come across a little church or, on leaving a lane, we find ourselves on a large square. Spatial structures and constellations are not merely seen and assessed, they are also sensed by the body. In this respect, existing studies would have to be reinterpreted.

Much the same applies to a domain that has so far been dominated by the discourse on signs, the domain that I would like to call the historical depth of a city. It is of course an enormous pleasure for the learned to be able to decipher a city, when its history becomes transparent through stylistic features, heraldry, epigraphs, and the materials employed. But these abilities can no longer be assumed to pertain to the average citizen, and historical information frequently denies the guided tourist the possibility of experiencing anything of the city. But 'being old' or 'having grown over time' are qualities of the city that do not manifest themselves solely in signs; rather, they make an impression (they have *Anmutungscharakter*) that is sensed. These could, perhaps, be the same qualities that can be read

One-way street: One of 2000 in Kyoto – places for life, 2005–7.

as signs, such as the ancient material or the ancient line of architecture, but they could also be completely different qualities. So, for example, we sense the historical depth of the city of Lübeck or Maastricht by the fact that the churches are, as it were, rooted: they rise, so to speak, from the ground, like trees. But we are also familiar with the disillusioning effect of the cleaning of the stained glass windows in Chartres cathedral. That is to say, inversely, that it is quite possible that a historical sign that suggests a distant epoch is not actually a reliable clue for divining the historical depth of a building. In this sense, faithful reconstruction can be as counterproductive as the removal of ivy from an old tower. The dimension of historical depth or the atmosphere of an organically developed city is, however, of major importance for the inhabitants' sense of feeling sheltered and at home.

In city planning, the acoustic dimension has so far been dealt with almost exclusively in quantitative terms – that is, with regard to noise pollution and its avoidance. The character of sounds has, on the other hand, almost never been a topic. The major exception here is August Endell, who in his book *Die Schönheit der großen Stadt,* under the heading 'The City of Sounds' (1908: 31–33), joyously pursues the manifold voices in the city of Berlin. However, I would like to let another witness – one who lived at the same time and in the same city – have his say: Victor Klemperer, in his *Curriculum Vitae.* I choose to quote him for the reason that in his text it is clear that the manner in which sounds are experienced in the city not only depends on decibels, but also on their character: 'I had found a room in Dennewitzstrasse. The house was very working class and not very hygienic. The windows opened onto the nearby railway embankment; the expanse of the rail network of the Anhalter and Potsdam stations unfolded there; day and night I was surrounded by the images, the many coloured lights, the rumbling and whistling, the cries and horn signals of the immense rolling stock. That touched me again and again like a wonderful promise' (1996, vol. 1: 401).

The worldwide project 'Soundscape' has done excellent preparatory work in researching the city as an acoustic space. In this project, it was composers and sound engineers, above all, who were concerned not only with the recording and composition of natural sounds but also

Children: Childcare is a great issue, 2005–7.

with the acoustic profile of cities. For example, one of the studies by the founder of Soundscape, Murray Schafer, dealt with the city of Vancouver. Soundscape researchers distinguished between an acoustic background (which, of course, continues to change throughout the day) and characteristic sound events.

In the interim, city planners have also taken up the topic. Thus, in his research for *La qualité sonore des espaces publiques Européens* (1995), Pascal Amphoux's particular perspective was determined by the hypothesis that the sound atmosphere of the city depends on national culture as well as the various forms of life. For this reason he studied, in the case of Switzerland, the sound atmospheres of Lausanne for the French region, Locarno for the Italian region, and Zurich for the German-speaking part.

The question of sound atmospheres is directly related to the dimension of lifestyles, understood as generators of urban atmospheres. In terms of street noise, it makes a difference whether it is customary for people to honk their horns or not, what type of car they drive, whether music can be heard through their open windows, whether the names of goods are shouted out, or whether 'alluring' music comes from the boutiques. These are just some aspects: through their lifestyles, the inhabitants of the city are also, always, producers of its atmosphere. Again, there is a literary witness for this – and once again it is Victor Klemperer. The city is Paris: 'In spite of the work, which for many daylight hours encapsulated me as if in an empty room, I remained constantly conscious of the Parisian atmosphere. This was already taken care of by the cheerful hustle and bustle in the small restaurants during lunch and dinner time, where at least one fat cat carelessly wandered between the feet of the guests and waiters on the sandy floor, one which probably caught a mouse occasionally and ate it quietly; and then the coffee counter, where you sometimes saw coachmen standing, the whips with the short handle and long strand thrown over their shoulders. Indeed, it seemed that my receptiveness to Parisian life grew with the intensity of my eagerness to work and with the shortage of time' (1996, vol. 2: 52).

Of course, I have chosen this text because it is also evidence of an early use of the term 'atmosphere' to designate the total impression that is regarded as characteristic of a city – in this case, Paris. Here, Klemperer condenses this impression and ties it to a particular scene, that of the small Parisian cafes and restaurants. In so doing, he refers to particular ingredients, like the sand strewn on the floor; he points out the nonchalance of the restaurant, in allowing cats inside; he sketches the fleeting presences of different types of people and their occupations (still identifiable at that time). We could, of course, add to this something from the novels of Zola, Proust, and Döblin, as well as from Walter Benjamin's unfinished study on the arcades of Paris.

The rule that we have to sense atmospheres applies especially to the atmospheres created by particular ways of living. In order to really get to know them, we ourselves have to enter into them fully, as it were. That is why film enjoys a certain advantage in communicating them. In fact, film often makes use of a particular urban atmosphere in order to generate the right atmosphere for a dramatic scene. A city atmosphere is very rarely, in itself, the subject of a film – Wim Wenders offering some of the few examples (Berlin, Tokyo, Lisbon).[1]

We can study the contribution of lifestyles to the development of the urban atmosphere, but they are not an object of planning. However, we can think about which measures in city development promote or prevent particular ways of living. Here we find a link with the critical studies of the modern city by psychologists and sociologists.

Conclusion

The concept of postmodernity comes from architectural theory. It served to indicate that something has come to an end in the development of architecture, namely modernism, which, especially for architecture, meant the domination of functionalism. For city planning, according to the Charter of Athens, this has meant a separation of the city's basic functions: residence, recreation, transportation, and work. It actually led to the desolation of inner cities, the intensification of commuter traffic, the development of satellite towns and city sprawl. The failure of this concept was made clear to architects and city planners by other professionals,

Cycle cemetery: Cycling is the most popular way to move around in the city, 2005–7.

Gernot Böhme

**Urban Atmospheres:
Charting New
Directions for
Architecture and
Urban Planning**

by psychologists and sociologists. However, innovation could not, strictly speaking, come from this side. Psychologists and sociologists have only the subjective factor at their disposal – at best, they could offer suggestions for compensatory measures to attenuate the mental and social harm done by modern city planning. For architects and city planners, the question is what concrete measures can change or develop cities in such a way that the mental and social harm criticised by psychologists and sociologists does not occur in the first place, and that life in the cities becomes tenable or even attractive. The necessary concepts and objectives have been specified, at least, in the discourse between architects and city planners and their critics. These are urbanisation, residential environment, identification possibilities, city image, staging the everyday world, and, more generally and correspondingly more vaguely, 'aesthetics'.

Here, the concept of atmosphere could first of all, and at least, change perception. It directs attention to the relation between the qualities of surroundings and dispositions (Böhme 1993). The atmosphere of a city is the subjective experience of urban reality that is shared by its people. They experience atmosphere as something objective, as a quality of the city. And it is indeed the case that, by analysing the generators of atmospheres from the point of view of the object (i.e. through city planning), we can bring about the conditions in which atmospheres of a particular character are able to develop. City planning's dimensions and possibilities for action are thereby extended; but so too, necessarily, is its attitude, for in the domain of atmospheres action does not always simply mean doing, it also means forbearance.

Footnotes

I Wim Wenders, *Tokyo-Ga*, 1984/85; *Wings of Desire*, 1987; *Far Away, So Close*, 1993, *Lisbon Story*, 1994.

References

Amphoux, Pascal. 1995. *Aux écoutes de la ville. La qualité sonore des espaces publiques européens – méthode d'analyse comparative – enquête sur trois villes Suisse.* Zurich: Schweizerischer Nationalfond.

Benjamin, Walter. 1973. 'The Work of Art in the Age of Mechanical Reproduction'. In *Illuminations*, translated by Harry Zohn. London: Fontana, 219–53.

Böhme, Gernot. 1993. *Für eine Ökologische Naturästhetik*, 3rd ed. Frankfurt am Main: Suhrkamp.

Böhme, Gernot. 2008. 'Die Atmosphäre'. In *Von der guten Form zum guten Leben*, edited by Michael Andritzky. Frankfurt am Main: Anabas-Verlag, 107–14.

Böhme, Gernot. 2013. *Atmosphäre. Essays zur neuen Ästhetik*, 7th ed. Frankfurt am Main: Suhrkamp.

Böhme, Gernot. 2011. 'Die Kunst des Bühnenbildes als Paradigma einer Ästhetik der Atmosphären'. In *Inszenierung und Vertrauen. Grenzgänge der Szenografie*, ed. by Ralf Bohn and Heiner Wilharm. Bielefeld: Transcript, 109–17. (English version: www. cresson.archi.fr/PUBLI/pubCOLL QUE/AMB8-confGBohme-eng.pdf)

Cullen, Gordon. 1968. *The Concise Townscape*, 5th ed. London: The Architectural Press.

Durth, Werner. 1988. *Die Inszenierung der Alltagswelt. Zur Kritik der Stadtgestaltung*, 2nd ed. Braunschweig and Wiesbaden: Vieweg.

Endell, August. 1908. *Die Schönheit der großen Stadt.* Stuttgart: Strecker und Schröder.

Hirschfeld, Christian Cajus Lorenz. 1779–85. *Theorie der Gartenkunst*, 5 vols. Leipzig: Weidmanns Erben und Reich.

Jencks, Charles. 1984. *The Language of Post-Modern Architecture*, 4th ed. London: Academy Editions.

Klemperer, Victor. 1996. *Curriculum Vitae. Erinnerungen 1881–1918*, 2 vols. Berlin: Aufbau.

Lynch, Kevin. 1960. *The Image of the City.* Cambridge, MA: MIT Press.

Norberg-Schulz, Christian. 1977. *Meaning in Western Architecture*, 3rd ed. New York: Praeger Publications.

Redner, Harry. 1994. *A New Science of Representation.* Boulder, CO: Westview.

Schmitz, Hermann. 2007. *Freiheit.* Freiburg and Munich: Karl Alber.

Christian Borch

**The Politics
of Atmospheres:
Architecture,
Power, and the
Senses**

In her brilliant book *The Transmission of Affect,* Teresa Brennan poses the following opening question: 'Is there anyone who has not, at least once, walked into a room and "felt the atmosphere"?' (Brennan 2004: 1). The experience of architecture to which Brennan points is familiar to most people: we are, perhaps unwittingly, aware of the particular characteristics of certain spaces – for example, the smells of our grandparents' home, the sounds of particular streets at certain times of the day, or the rhythms and sensory impressions of entire villages or urban districts. For Brennan, what is interesting about such phenomena is how the '"atmosphere" or environment literally gets into the individual' (2004: 1). She suggests that when more people are present in the same locale, and hence share the same atmosphere, a transmission of affect may take place, in which the affective state of one person transmits contagiously to the others, meaning that the social situation in effect changes the biological constitution of each individual.

The idea that co-presence in a particular locale can mould individuals' affective states immediately raises questions relating to *power and politics* – although, interestingly, these are not among Brennan's explicit concerns. Yet the powerful and political aspects of atmospheres have received considerable attention in other recent social theory. For example, Gernot Böhme has convincingly argued for studying not just how atmospheres are experienced, but also how these experiences and their emotional effects may be strategically produced, designed, and staged (see Böhme's article in this volume). Among other things, Böhme has discussed the politically motivated design of atmospheres with reference to Nazi architecture and Hitler's orchestration of mass events (2006: 162–72). I will return to Böhme's work later in this essay, the aim of which is to examine the politics of (architectural) atmospheres. First, however, I would like to discuss an alternative approach to the politics of atmospheres, namely the one proposed by another German philosopher, Peter Sloterdijk. In his *Spheres* trilogy, Sloterdijk provides a new foundation for discussing space, architecture, and politics, and their interrelations. In the first part of the essay, I will discuss the fundamental tenets of Sloterdijk's spherology. In the second part, I will proceed to how the spherological perspective invites an examination of atmospheric politics, i.e. the attempt to manage behaviour through interventions in the physical and/or socio-psychic environment. I will use this discussion as a stepping-stone for advancing an argument that extends beyond Sloterdijk's own concerns and reflections. Thus, as I will suggest in the third part, in which I discuss the relations between atmospheres and the senses, the politics of atmospheres may well operate in more profound ways than Sloterdijk envisages. Indeed, I argue, that atmospheric design may work on a non-conscious level. In other words, when architectural atmospheres are created so as to affect us through the senses, atmospheric design operates in ways that we barely recognise consciously. Accordingly, and this is the central claim of this essay, the design of architectural atmospheres might be seen as a subtle form of power, in which behaviour, desires, and experiences are governed or managed without people being consciously aware of this. In making this argument, I refer to some of Böhme's and Brennan's ideas.[1]

Spheres, Atmospheres, Immunity As mentioned above, the notion of atmospheres has received ample attention in social theory in recent years, where it has been deployed to account for both architectural and non-architectural phenomena (e.g. Anderson 2009; Heibach 2012; Knodt 1994; Philippopoulos-Mihalopoulos 2013). Yet theoretical reflections on atmospheres date further back. In a philosophical context the concept of atmospheres is associated in particular with Hermann Schmitz's 1969 book *Der Gefühlsraum,* in which the notion of atmospheres was detached from a metrological understanding and conceived instead in broader terms as moods (*Stimmungen*) that are spatially discharged (Schmitz 1969). Böhme's work on atmospheres is indebted to this phenomenological conception, although it also goes beyond it by analysing how atmospheres are not merely experienced but also deliberately produced (e.g. Böhme 2006). Next to Schmitz and Böhme, the most original recent discussion of atmospheres is the one presented by Peter Sloterdijk.

In his magnum opus *Spheres,* published in three volumes in German in 1998, 1999, and 2004 (but still only partially available in English translation), Sloterdijk puts forward a comprehensive reconceptualisation of human being, emphasising its embeddedness in spatial configurations. Sloterdijk calls these spatial configurations *spheres,* defined as

Urban atmospheres. Eugène Atget, *The Panthéon,* 1924. Gelatin silver chloride print on printing-out paper, 17.8 × 22.6 cm. The J. Paul Getty Museum, Los Angeles.

Urban atmospheres. Eugène Atget, *The Old School of Medicine, rue de la Bucherie,* 1898. Albumen silver print, 21 × 17.6 cm. The J. Paul Getty Museum, Los Angeles.

'the interior, disclosed, shared realm inhabited by humans – in so far as they succeed in becoming humans' (2011: 28). The basic assertion underpinning Sloterdijk's project is that such spheres provide people with meaning, community, and a sense of immunity (or protection, security), whether in a material, social, or more ideational sense. For example, architecture (a house, an apartment, etc.) may constitute a material sphere that offers a sense of meaning and safety for its inhabitants, i.e. a place where they feel at home in all senses of the term. Likewise, ideology and religion are examples of ideational spheres in which people acquire a sense of belonging to a meaningful and essentially protective community. Sloterdijk's point is both that sustaining a life independently of any sphere(s) is simply impossible and that the actual forms that spheres assume may materialise in highly different structures. To demonstrate the latter point, each of the three volumes of *Spheres* focuses on its own spherological level.

The first volume is entitled, in English translation, *Bubbles: Microspherology* (2011). This book presents an exploration of the most intimate socio-spatial relations, the so-called dual bubbles that refer to the 'dyadic space of resonance between people as we find it in symbiotic relations' such as those of mother and child, teacher and student, hypnotiser and hypnotised, etc. (Funcke 2005; Sloterdijk 2011: 67). One of the crucial points of the microspherological analysis is that it zeroes in on dyadic relations, rather than taking its analytical starting point in the singular individual. For Sloterdijk, human beings are not free-floating islands, but are nested together in particular socio-spatial configurations. Indeed, his analysis suggests that one only becomes an individual on the basis of a co-subjective couple relation. The second volume, *Globen: Makrosphärologie* [Globes: Macrospheorology], performs a radical change of perspective (Sloterdijk 1999). Rather than examining tiny, dyadic microspheres, it focuses on the kinds of spheres that function as a protective membrane on a more global scale. Examples include ancient Greek cosmology and Christian theology, but one may add to this list all sorts of nationalism and grand political ideologies (regardless of their particular leaning). The central claim here is that each of these global spheres provided a comprehensive understanding of the world, i.e. it offered the people gathered within it a sense of shared meaning and immunity.

Christian Borch

**The Politics
of Atmospheres:
Architecture,
Power, and the
Senses**

However, Sloterdijk adds – and this is why global spheres are referred to in the past tense – (post)modern society has rendered such global meta-physical spheres fundamentally unconvincing. Instead, Sloterdik argues, we are currently living in a social order that is best described through the notion of foam. The third volume of the *Spheres* trilogy, *Schäume: Plurale Sphärologie* [Foams: Plural Spherology], therefore aims to come to terms with the foaming nature of the contemporary world (Sloterdijk 2004).

Sloterdijk conceives of foam as a highly complex, even chaotic, acentric agglomeration of bubbles. Inspired by the American architectural group Morphosis and their notion of 'connected isolations', Sloterdijk defines foam as consisting of 'co-isolated associations' of bubbles (2004: 255). Drawing on this image, he describes the present foam sociality as follows: '[It is] an aggregate of microspheres (couples, households, com-panies, associations) of different formats that are adjacent to one another like individual bubbles in a mound of foam and are structured one layer over/under the other, without really being accessible to or separable from one another' (Sloterdijk 2004: 59).

As the quote makes clear, when accounting for the social, Sloterdijk deliberately alludes to foam as a physical substance. The image of a lather best characterises the modern social world: we all inhabit minor, bubbling worlds of our own – or 'households', as Sloterdijk (2004: 55) calls them. These worlds may be related in certain ways (for instance, when neigh-bouring bubbles share the same membrane), but they do not overlap. Consequently, the social foam as a whole has no shared meaning and no common sense of protection; rather, meanings and immunity have a much more particularistic anchoring.[2]

While most of this may sound highly abstract, Sloterdijk discusses the spherological aspects of foam sociality through a number of concrete examples, and much of that discussion centres on the importance of architecture. For example, in line with the notion that spheres provide protection, Sloterdijk suggests that a residence constitutes a 'spatial immune system' (2004: 535). In other words, a house or an apartment of-fers its inhabitants physical protection against the outer world. This may materialise as a particular sense of homeliness, as when people feel that

Atmospheres of abandonment. Jeanne Fredac, *Badezimmer,* 2011, Berlin.

Christian Borch

The Politics
of Atmospheres:
Architecture,
Power, and the
Senses

the residence constitutes a relaxing and comfortable 'backstage' (Goffman 1959: 114) to their public life. However, it may also materialise in a more directly protective manner – for example, when people conceive of the walls of their residence as a physical bulwark against actual or perceived threats (violence, assaults, etc.) from outside. Sloterdijk's emphasis on the immunological nature of spheres entails that his perspective is more attuned to the protective dimension (Borch 2013b). Indeed, he describes a residence as 'immunologically speaking, a defensive measure designed to demarcate a sphere of well-being from invaders and other agents of unwellness' (2004: 535).

The emphasis on the defensive side of architecture finds an equivalent expression in Sloterdijk's fascination with the American designer and architect Richard Buckminster Fuller. What particularly interests Sloterdijk about Buckminster Fuller's work is the latter's mobile architecture. In the late 1920s, Buckminster Fuller famously invented the Dymaxion House, a new type of 'industrially-to-be-produced, service-rented, air-deliverable, scientific dwelling machines' (Buckminster Fuller 1981: 138; see also Sieden 1989: 271–85). These fully-equipped, easily-erected, mobile one-family houses were seen by Buckminster Fuller as a means of ensuring affordable housing for all parts of the population, as well as of making workers in particular less vulnerable to the vagaries of the economy – the vulnerability consisting of being hired in one (perhaps even remote) place, buying a house there, losing one's job in times of economic decline, and finding oneself stuck, with little flexibility with regard to selling the house and moving elsewhere. Much like a snail shell, the Dymaxion house could be disassembled, moved, and reassembled at a new and more prosperous location. In Sloterdijk's terms, such mobile architecture amounts to a singular sphere which, cast in the big mould of social foam, offers immunity, not so much through thick protective walls, but rather via its mobility, i.e. its high adaptability and independence of a particular locale.

This is but one type of architecture examined by Sloterdijk. Other related analyses focus on more permanent forms of architecture that give material expression to the foamy modality of the present. Such architectures include, in generic form, apartment blocks in which each

Atmospheres of future consumption. Jeanne Fredac, *Zukünftiger Supermarkt*, 2011, Berlin.

Urban atmospheres. Eugène Atget, *Luxembourg Gardens,* 1902–3. Albumen silver print, 17.5 × 22.1 cm. The J. Paul Getty Museum, Los Angeles.

apartment constitutes its own bubble, which shares membranes with the neighbouring apartments. As Sloterdijk notes, such apartments need not provide total immunity towards neighbours, since noises and smells may well permeate the walls, meaning that particular kinds of connected isolation are at work here (2004: 577). Further, Sloterdijk argues that the present foam sociality is reflected in the work of particular contemporary architects. One is Renzo Piano's transformation of the Lingotto building in Torino, Italy, the roof of which features a transparent, domed meeting room, appropriately called the 'bubble' (2004: 649, 651). Another example is Elizabeth Diller and Ricardo Scofidio's Blur Building from the Swiss 2002 Expo, which, for Sloterdijk, amounts to a contemporary form of 'atmo-architecture' (2004: 668–70).

It would be easy to point to other examples from contemporary architecture in which bubbling, foamy shapes predominate – from blob architecture (Lynn 1999) to PTW Architects' National Swimming Centre in Beijing, to mention just two. However, for present purposes, I am more interested in the more general analytical aspects of Sloterdijk's approach. As intimated above, what the sphere perspective offers is a way of addressing that human being always takes place in particular spatial configurations – not in the simple sense that space (like time) is an unavoidable given, but in the more ontological and existential sense that some form of meaning and immunity is required for human beings to sustain themselves. This is achieved through particular spatial embeddings – namely, specific spheres that may take the form of dyadic bubbles, globes, or co-isolated foam structures. In itself, however, this understanding does not entail any reflections on the politics of (atmo)spheres. And yet, as I will discuss below, Sloterdijk's *Schäume* actually contains several analyses that do indeed lay out a novel conception of atmospheric politics.

Atmospheric Politics Sloterdijk has two general approaches to atmospheric politics. One relates to his analysis of so-called airquakes, which refer to a series of significant twentieth-century events in which human beings' dependency on specific air conditions became the object of close analytical scrutiny and political attention. In particular, Sloterdijk emphasises gas warfare as a key illustration of this (2004: 89–153). Therefore,

Christian Borch

**The Politics
of Atmospheres:
Architecture,
Power, and the
Senses**

when the German army attacked the French with poison gas at Ypres on 22 April 1915, this amounted to a profound transformation in the nature of warfare with grave consequences. Rather than seeking to target the bodies of the enemy soldiers, their *environment* – including, in a very concrete sense, the air they breathed – now gained increasing attention as a point of strategic military intervention. Put differently, what emerged here, according to Sloterdijk, was a particular kind of atmospheric politics that pivoted around the atmosphere (or air conditions, broadly understood) – the aim was to attack the individuals through the atmosphere they share.

For Sloterdijk, gas warfare constituted the first central twentieth-century airquake, directed as it was against the physical air conditions of soldiers. At more or less the same time, another, more socio-psychological airquake materialised with the emergence of large-scale media propaganda. The target of mass-media propaganda is not so much to modify the air people breathe, but rather to exercise power over people by controlling the circulation of information. This medial politics of atmospheres, too, can have important consequences. Indeed, Sloterdijk suggests, '[l]ife in the media state resembles a sojourn in a palace filled with gas, animated by the poisons of themed events' (2004: 187).

Combined, these two types of airquakes resemble what Böhme arrives at in his analysis of Nazi architecture. In contradistinction to Walter Benjamin's famous thesis about how Fascism marked 'the introduction of aesthetics into political life' (Benjamin 2007: 241), Böhme argues that the really significant feature of Hitler's regime was how it not merely aestheticised the political, but how its political strategies were also based on the deliberate manipulation of previously non-politicised fields and objects. More precisely, Hitler simply expunged the boundaries between the political and the non-political, as practically everything could be utilised for political purposes. Drawing on Hermann Schmitz, Böhme suggests that this materialised in a political strategy aimed at comprehensive 'impressions engineering' [*Eindruckstechnik*], which included the use of posters, radio propaganda, movies, mass meetings, etc. (Böhme 2006: 165). The Nazi mass meetings in particular reflected a combination of physical-architectural and socio-psychological air conditioning, as

Sloterdijk would put it. Hitler himself was rather explicit about this. In *Mein Kampf,* he devoted great energy to discussing how to render media propaganda most effective (Borch 2013a; see also 2012). Among other things, Hitler argued that the spoken word was better suited for propaganda purposes than written media because, he believed, it was more difficult for the receiver to ignore speech on the radio than to skip one or more pages in the newspaper. The validity (or not) of this claim is not important in the present context. More central are Hitler's reflections on why mass-mediated propaganda (i.e. socio-psychological air conditioning) should be complemented with mass meetings (and hence with more physical air conditioning). He reasoned that every kind of mass-media propaganda faces the obstacle that it might be aimed at people who hold opposing views. Moving such people to subscribe to one's own propaganda can be highly difficult, Hitler believed, especially since propaganda is not about rational arguments but about emotions. This is where the orchestration of physical mass meetings was attributed vital importance by Hitler. The effect of such physical-architectural staging would be that, when a person: 'steps for the first time into a mass meeting and has thousands and thousands of people of the same opinions around him, when, as a seeker, he is swept away by three or four thousand others into the mighty effect of suggestive intoxication and enthusiasm, when the visible success and agreement of thousands confirm to him the rightness of the new doctrine and for the first time arouse doubt in the truth of his previous conviction – then he himself has succumbed to the magic influence of what we might designate as "mass suggestion"' (Hitler 1992: 435).

In other words, Hitler believed that designing huge mass events would provide the best conditions for effective propaganda. Creating an architectural setting in which people could assemble physically and feel the sense of a shared sphere would, according to this line of thought, render it increasingly attractive to be part of the spherological community. This, in turn, would remove any prior obstacles to the propaganda being disseminated at the mass event. Interestingly, Hitler went on to suggest that the propaganda would be most efficient if the mass meetings were organised at night – when, allegedly, people experience a natural 'weakening of their force of resistance' (1992: 432). According to Hitler, a

French President Charles de Gaulle travels by car down the Champs Elysees on
Bastille Day (14 July) 1968.

similar atmospheric effect was achieved in the religious domain 'by the artificially made and yet mysterious twilight in Catholic churches, the burning lamps, incense, censers, etc.' (1992: 432).

While the Hitler regime put great emphasis on such mass events and their politico-atmospheric staging, it did not invent them. As Sloterdijk points out in *Sphären III: Schäume,* the entire modern political order was born as mass orchestration. Sloterdijk illustrates this with a reference to an early path-defining example from France, namely the so-called Fête de la Fédération of 14 July 1790, which was organised to celebrate the first anniversary of the storming of the Bastille. This celebration was born out of the grand ambition to create a space 'where not only the representatives could meet, but also those represented, namely the crowd of the [sovereign] people' (Sloterdijk 2008: 52). The Fête de la Fédération was organised in Paris at the Champs de Mars, where about 400,000 people reportedly gathered to celebrate the Revolution. What is particularly significant about this event is how it prefigured the Hitler era's melding of physical and socio-psychological air conditioning. At this point, it is worth quoting at length Sloterdijk's account of the Fête de la Fédération: 'The reborn circus [of the Fête de la Fédération], as political focus and as *fascinogenic* mass collector, comprises a machine to produce consensus, and thus the directors of the ritual must ensure that all processes in it are elementarily comprehensible. Anyone who does not understand the text must grasp the action; anyone for whom the action is alien must be captivated by the colourfulness of the spectacle. The rest is cared for by sonospheric melding. In this situation, the so-called sovereign can never directly speak; however, it can applaud its representatives when they take the stage and can in fact, if it so wishes, go one step further, and by cheering and screaming transform itself into an acoustic we-phenomenon *sui generis.* Where discrete coordination is not possible, the collective that roars itself hoarse has results of psycho-political relevance. The quasination assembled in the circus/stadium experiences itself in an acoustic plebiscite, the direct result of which, the jubilatory noise that rises above everyone's heads, breaks forth from the assembled qua emanation and returns to the ears of each individually. The autopoiesis of noise approximates the realisation of the cliché of the *vox populi.* Such roaring

People dance in the streets as a celebration of Bastille Day in Paris, France, c. 1940.

[...] renders rhetoric on the part of individual speakers superfluous. Via mimetic infection, the shout by the one becomes the shout by the other' (2008: 54–55, italics in original).

There are several important things to note here. One is how, in a modern Western context, political mass production is intimately tied to the aesthetic and architectural politics of atmospheres. Once again, this is nicely captured by Sloterdijk, when he states that: 'The preparation and implementation of the Fête de la Fédération of 1790 and subsequent events make it evident that the "mass", the "nation" or the "people" as a collective subject can only exist to the extent that the physical assembling of these quantities is the object of artful orchestration – from mobilisation through participation to directed effects in a stadium and the enthralling of "mass" attention by *fascinogenic* spectacles – right through to the civil guard breaking up the crowd on its way home' (2008: 54, italics in original).

Another important dimension relates to how, as intimated above, the Fête de la Fédération introduced a novel kind of *sensory politics.* The socio-psychological sphere that was believed to emerge at the mass event was one that was at once expressed through and produced by sensory design – not least via acoustic means. That is, the acoustic we-phenomenon to which Sloterdijk refers emerges on the basis of, and as a result of, the particular atmo-political spectacle that was organised. This suggests that Sloterdijk's analysis of the Fête de la Fédération points at the intersection of atmospheric politics and sensory manipulation. But how do these relate more specifically?

Atmospheres and the Senses As many have argued, modernity (and Western culture, more generally) has privileged vision over the other senses. For example, scholars such as David Michael Levin (1993) have demonstrated how modern knowledge has been intimately tied to vision: knowing means seeing. Similarly, conceptions of power often lay bare a distinctive ocularcentrism. For instance, Nikolas Rose, taking inspiration from Michel Foucault and Bruno Latour, suggests that: 'To govern, it is necessary to render visible the space over which government is to be exercised. This is not simply a matter of looking; it is a practice by which

Christian Borch

**The Politics
of Atmospheres:
Architecture,
Power, and the
Senses**

the space is re-presented in maps, charts, pictures and other inscription devices' (1999: 37).

Further, it is argued that the exercise of power is conditioned by seeing and making things observable. Interestingly, even the field of architecture has been accused of placing undue emphasis on vision. Most notably, perhaps, Juhani Pallasmaa has lamented the tendency within architecture and urban planning to privilege vision, such that buildings and city plans are 'turned into image products detached from existential depth and sincerity' (1995: 30). In opposition to this trend, Pallasmaa makes a plea for 'a sensory architecture', i.e. a way of conceiving, teaching, critiquing, and practising architecture that takes into account its haptic, acoustic, aromatic, etc. aspects (1995: 39; see also 2009; 2011). What emerges here is, one might add, a call for an atmospheric notion of architecture. Not surprisingly, Pallasmaa praises the architect Peter Zumthor, who explicitly subscribes to an atmospheric approach (Zumthor 2006), for producing 'a multitude of sensory experiences' in his work (Pallasmaa 1995: 70). While much of Pallasmaa's work centres on how adopting an atmospheric viewpoint produces important insights into the existential dimensions of architecture, it also invites a discussion of the *political* implications of atmospheric design. As I will argue in the following, the production of architectural atmospheres amounts to a subtle form of power that aims to achieve its effects by working on a non-conscious level. In other words, the design of architectural atmospheres calls for critical analysis not least because it seeks to govern behaviour, desires, and experiences without people necessarily being consciously aware of this.

To understand this, it is helpful to return to the work of Böhme and Brennan. As mentioned above, Brennan takes as her starting point a person entering a room and feeling its atmosphere. Brennan argues that when people share a space, one person's affective state (anxiety, joy, etc.) can be transmitted to others without them necessarily being consciously aware of this. According to Brennan, this transmission takes place through processes of entrainment, where, for example, people breathe in or consume – and are thereby affected by – pheromones secreted by other individuals. One central corollary of this is that Brennan entirely dissolves the idea of the individual self as contained by his or her skin. This idea

78

Producing urban atmospheres. Olafur Eliasson, *Double sunset,* 1999. Installation view at Panorama, Utrecht, 2000.

Christian Borch

The Politics
of Atmospheres:
Architecture,
Power, and the
Senses

is replaced by the notion that the self is constantly exposed to and in interaction with its environment, also in a bodily-affective sense. Indeed, Brennan concludes from her example, the 'affect *in the room* is a profoundly social thing' (2004: 68, italics in original). If, for instance, the room is laden with anxiety, then the affective state of a person entering the room will likely be changed as he or she unwittingly breathes in the smell of anxiety. Importantly, Brennan's analysis particularly emphasises the role of the senses in the transmission of affect: pheromones are detected mainly through touch or smell, but she also argues that entrainment may take place as well through auditory and visual media (2004: 70–71).

Brennan's perspective offers an understanding of how what one person feels in a certain room is intimately tied to other persons' affective state. As such, even if the process through which affective states are coupled works at the level of chemical entrainment, the basic thrust of Brennan's analysis is to explain affect as essentially *social*. This is all interesting and important, but it may be argued that Brennan's example of the person feeling the atmosphere of a room pays insufficient attention to *the room itself* and how it, too, participates in creating the particular atmosphere. In short, Brennan disregards the architectural aspects of atmospheres. Here Böhme's work is of help.

Böhme defines atmospheres as 'tuned spaces or [...] spatially discharged, quasi-objective feelings' (2006: 16). The central point here is that a room produces a certain feeling, which is felt more or less similarly regardless of who experiences it. For example, the Holocaust Tower in Daniel Libeskind's Jewish Museum in Berlin produces an oppressing atmosphere that any visitor is likely to feel. As such, it assumes a quasi-objective – i.e. not subjectively bound – quality. Much less radical examples are, of course, legion, and can be identified in any kind of architecture. Indeed, every encounter with architecture contains the possibility that we are being seized by its atmosphere, even if some atmospheres (such as the Holocaust Tower) are felt more intensely than others. Importantly, Böhme is not suggesting any determinism here. Entering a room and feeling its atmosphere does not entail that one's state of being (*Befindlichkeit*) is determined by the room's qualities. It is more correct to say that a person's basic mood (i.e. the mood, or *Grundstimmung,* in which he or she enters the room) is influenced or affected by the atmosphere of the room (Böhme 2006: 122).

Böhme's notion of atmospheres takes us back to the sensory domain, as he particularly emphasises the role of the senses in how atmospheres are experienced. In a discussion of urban atmospheres, he observes that 'smells are a crucial element of a city's atmosphere, perhaps even the most crucial one, for smells are atmospheric to a greater degree than other sensory phenomena' (2006: 128). Böhme illustrates this by describing how, for him, the atmosphere of Paris used to be associated with the particular smell of subway stations. Much like Marcel Proust's protagonist, consuming that smell in another context would immediately remind him of the Parisian subway. This ties in nicely with Pallasmaa's observation that 'the most persistent memory of any space is often its smell' (1995: 54). Böhme attributes particular importance to the olfactory dimension, but he also addresses other senses in his examinations of atmospheres. For example, vision is analysed in discussions of how the atmospheres of ecclesiastical spaces are based on particular uses of light (Böhme 1998: 85–104). Similarly, hearing is linked to atmospheres in discussions of how, for instance, shops use Muzak (alongside olfactory manipulation) to entice customers to stay longer and consume more, as well as how particular soundscapes and specific acoustic qualities characterise certain cities and regions (Böhme 1998: 71–84, as well as his article in this volume; see also Augoyard and Torgue 2005; Schafer 1971).

There are two important points to be made in continuation of this. First, architectural atmospheres cannot be seen as pure emergence, i.e. as something that arises more or less out of the blue and captures people. Quite the contrary, as mentioned several times above, atmospheres are often *produced.* Indeed, artists often focus on creating particular atmospheres so as to induce particular kinds of experiences and behaviours and/or to stimulate debate. Prominent examples of this can be found in the work of Olafur Eliasson, who often endows his installations with a decidedly atmospheric dimension. His 2003 installation *The weather project* at Tate Modern in London is probably the most famous illustration of this, but the production of urban and other atmospheres are also

Christian Borch

**The Politics
of Atmospheres:
Architecture,
Power, and the
Senses**

visible in many of his other projects – including *Double sunset* (1999), where an artificial sun was erected in Utrecht in the Netherlands to simulate the impression of a second sunset, and *Your blind passenger* (2010), which invites the spectator into a tunnel of thick fog, where their sense of direction is lost due to heavy air conditioning. Similarly, architecture as a practice (as opposed to merely its aesthetic adaptations) also focuses on the production of atmospheres. In the words of Böhme: '[a]rchitecture produces atmospheres in everything it creates. Of course, it also solves specific problems and fabricates objects and buildings of all sorts. But architecture is aesthetic work in the sense that it always also generates spaces with a special mood quality, i.e. atmospheres. [...] The visitor, the user, the customer, the patient are met with or seized by these atmospheres. The architect, however, creates them, more or less consciously' (1995: 97).

While Böhme rightly points out that architects may not always be consciously aware of the atmospheric dimensions of their work, including how particular architectures produce atmospheres that make certain feelings and modes of behaviour more likely than others, I hope that the above discussions of Sloterdijk and Böhme have demonstrated that, very often, architectural atmospheres are carefully and consciously designed in order to achieve specific political objectives. Something similar applies, perhaps even to a greater extent, to the economic domain. Back in the early 1970s, the marketing professor Philip Kotler coined the term 'atmospherics' to designate a new field of research and practical intervention which revolved around the idea that '[i]n some cases, the place, more specifically the *atmosphere* of the place, is more influential than the product itself in the purchase decision. In some cases, the atmosphere is the primary product' (Kotler 1973–74: 48, italics in original). Accordingly, Kotler argued in favour of making the design of atmospheres a central element in marketing, a call subsequently taken up by a whole field, referred to as hospitality management, which studies how, for example, hotel atmospheres can be generated to enhance customer satisfaction (e.g. Heide and Grønhaug 2006; Heide and Grønhaug 2009; Heide, Lærdal and Grønhaug 2009). Such work is in perfect alignment with Kotler's ambitions since, for him, '*atmospherics* is the effort to design buying

Producing urban atmospheres. Olafur Eliasson, *Double sunset,* 1999. Installation view at Panorama, Utrecht, 2000.

Air conditioning through art. Olafur Eliasson, *Din blinde passager,* 2010. Installation view at ARKEN Museum for Moderne Kunst, 2010.

environments to produce specific emotional effects in the buyer that enhance his [sic] purchase ability' (Kotler 1973–74: 50, italics in original).

Second, the fact that atmospheres have a strong sensory component entails that designing architectural atmospheres amounts to a form of sensory power, if power is conceived as per Michel Foucault: 'The exercise of power is a "conduct of conducts" and a management of possibilities', i.e. power is a way 'to structure the possible field of action of others' (Foucault 2001: 341). This notion of power is highly pertinent to an understanding of atmospheric-sensory design. According to Jim Drobnick: 'Researchers have shown that a pleasant odor elevates the mood of patrons, improves a store's image, enriches the evaluations of products, increases the time consumers spend in a store and their intention to return and, most importantly, boosts both the price shoppers are willing to pay for a product and the amount of spending in a store overall' (2006: 346).

Obviously, none of this would be the case if people were consciously aware of being subjected to sensory design. As such, what emerges here is the notion that power is being exercised without people recognising its operations: staging architectural atmospheres through sensory design constitutes a 'conduct of conduct', in which quasi-objective feelings are being produced that people need not recognise consciously, but which nevertheless affect their behaviour. Compared to other forms of power, a politics of atmospheres (or atmospheric 'conduct of conduct') assumes a subtle form, precisely because it works on a non-conscious level. Again, no determinism is at play here. There is no guarantee that all people, at all times, will act as is hoped for (Löw 2008). And yet, as the Drobnick quote makes plain, there is evidence that atmospheric-sensory design actually does achieve some intended practical effects. Furthermore, even if such effects may not completely correspond to the intentions behind the atmospheric design, it remains important to bring to the fore and analyse how such design is not merely a matter of producing, say, comfortable or exciting spaces, but also about conditioning experiences and rendering some behaviours more likely than others. In short, atmospheric design is intimately tied to power.

Christian Borch

The Politics
of Atmospheres:
Architecture,
Power, and the
Senses

Conclusion As this essay has demonstrated, there are different ways to address and conceptualise the relation between architecture and atmospheres. Common to the perspectives discussed above is the notion that architectural atmospheres should be analysed with a view to power and politics. In other words, an atmospheric approach to architecture does not simply amount to a call for a particular type of (multisensory) aesthetic awareness; it also amounts to taking seriously that (and how) architecture affects us, and that (and how) this occurs through its atmospheric dimensions. To extrapolate from Sloterdijk's ideas, it may be said that we are dependent on atmospheres: the air we breathe and the spaces we inhabit are formative for our existence as human beings. People use atmospheres as shells that offer protection and make sense of the world. However, the immunity granted by atmospheres may come at a price, as it is often embedded in larger objectives of governing behaviours, experiences, and desires – whether this materialises in the economic field, in attempts to entice consumers to spend more money, or politically, in the form of mobilising support or deterring certain types of behaviour. This is another way of saying that architecture has long since lost its innocence – or, more accurately, that it never was innocent. The particular advantage of pursuing an atmospheric approach to architecture therefore lies in recognising that architecture should not be subsumed under a merely aesthetic discourse. Architectural atmospheres affect us, change our moods, and influence our behaviours, and these effects may be produced without us consciously recognising them. The fact that there is a lack of scholarly attention directed towards the numerous ways in which an architectural atmospheric 'conduct of conduct' is exercised should only encourage further inquiries into the politics of atmospheres.

Air conditioning through art. Olafur Eliasson, *Din blinde passager,* 2010. Installation view at ARKEN Museum for Moderne Kunst, 2010.

Footnotes

1 Throughout the essay I draw on some of my previous work on Sloterdijk and Böhme, especially Borch (2008; 2013b).

2 This does not entail that meaning and immunity only exist locally, in a physical-spatial sense. Sloterdijk stresses that neighbouring bubbles refer to 'the users of analogous immunisation strategies, of identical patterns of creativity, of related arts of survival; meaning that most "neighbours" live far apart and resemble one another only in terms of imitative infections (which are now termed "trans-cultural exchange")' (2004: 259).

References

Anderson, Ben. 2009. 'Affective Atmospheres'. *Emotion, Space and Society* 2: 77–81.

Augoyard, Jean-François, and Henry Torgue. 2005. *Sonic Experience: A Guide to Everyday Sounds.* Montreal: McGill-Queen's University Press.

Benjamin, Walter. 2007. 'The Work of Art in the Age of Mechanical Reproduction'. In *Illuminations,* translated by Harry Zohn. New York: Schocken Books, 217–51.

Borch, Christian. 2008. 'Foam Architecture: Managing Co-Isolated Associations'. *Economy and Society* 37 (4): 548–71.

Borch, Christian. 2012. *The Politics of Crowds: An Alternative History of Sociology.* Cambridge: Cambridge University Press.

Borch, Christian. 2013a. 'Crowd Theory and the Management of Crowds: A Controversial Relationship'. *Current Sociology* 61 (5–6): 584–601.

Borch, Christian. 2013b. 'Spatiality, Imitation, Immunisation: Luhmann and Sloterdijk on the Social'. In *Luhmann Observed: Radical Theoretical Encounters,* edited by Anders La Cour and Andreas Philippopoulos-Mihalopoulos. Houndmills, Basingstoke: Palgrave Macmillan, 150–68.

Brennan, Teresa. 2004. *The Transmission of Affect.* Ithaca and London: Cornell University Press.

Buckminster Fuller, Richard. 1981. *Critical Path.* New York: St. Martin's Press.

Böhme, Gernot. 1995. *Atmosphäre. Essays zur neuen Ästhetik.* Frankfurt am Main: Suhrkamp.

Böhme, Gernot. 1998. *Anmutungen. Über das Atmosphärische.* Ostfildern vor Stuttgart: Edition Tertium, Arcaden.

Böhme, Gernot. 2006. *Architektur und Atmosphäre.* Munich: Wilhelm Fink.

Drobnick, Jim. 2006. 'Eating Nothing: Cooking Aromas in Art and Culture', In *The Smell Culture Reader,* edited by Jim Drobnick. Oxford and New York: Berg, 342–56.

Foucault, Michel. 2001. 'The Subject and Power'. In *Essential Works of Michel Foucault,* vol. 3, *Power,* edited by James D. Faubion. London: Penguin Books, 326–48.

Funcke, Bettina. 2005. 'Against Gravity: Bettina Funcke Talks with Peter Sloterdijk'. *Bookforum* (Feb / Mar).

Goffman, Erving. 1959. *The Presentation of Self in Everyday Life.* London: Penguin Books.

Heibach, Christiane, ed. 2012. *Atmosphären. Dimensionen eines diffusen Phänomens.* Munich: Wilhelm Fink.

Heide, Morten, and Kjell Grønhaug. 2006. 'Atmosphere: Conceptual Issues and Implications for Hospitality Management'. *Scandinavian Journal of Hospitality and Tourism* 6 (4): 271–86.

Heide, Morten, and Kjell Grønhaug. 2009. 'Key Factors in Guests' Perception of Hotel Atmosphere'. *Cornell Hospitality Quarterly* 50 (1): 29–43.

Heide, Morten, Kirsti Lærdal, and Kjell Grønhaug. 2009. 'Atmosphere as a Tool for Enhancing Organizational Performance: An Exploratory Study from the Hospitality Industry'. *European Journal of Marketing* 43 (3–4): 305–19.

Hitler, Adolf. 1992. *Mein Kampf,* translated by Ralph Manheim. London: Pimlico.

Knodt, Reinhard. 1994. *Ästhetische Korrespondenzen. Denken im technischen Raum.* Stuttgart: Philipp Reclam.

Kotler, Philip. 1973–74. 'Atmospherics as a Marketing Tool'. *Journal of Retailing* 49 (4): 48–64.

Levin, David Michael, ed. 1993. *Modernity and the Hegemony of Vision.* Berkeley, CA: University of California Press.

Lynn, Greg. 1999. *Animate Form.* New York: Princeton Architectural Press.

Löw, Martina. 2008. 'The Constitution of Space: The Structuration of Spaces Through the Simultaneity of Effect and Perception'. *European Journal of Social Theory* 11 (1): 25–49.

Pallasmaa, Juhani. 1995. *The Eyes of the Skin: Architecture and the Senses.* Chichester: John Wiley & Sons.

Pallasmaa, Juhani. 2009. *The Thinking Hand: Existential and Embodied Wisdom in Architecture.* Chichester: John Wiley & Sons.

Pallasmaa, Juhani. 2011. *The Embodied Image: Imagination and Imagery in Architecture.* Chichester: John Wiley & Sons.

Philippopoulos-Mihalopoulos, Andreas. 2013. 'Atmospheres of Law: Senses, Affects, Lawscapes'. *Emotion, Space and Society* 7: 35–44.

Rose, Nikolas. 1999. *Powers of Freedom: Reframing Political Thought.* Cambridge: Cambridge University Press.

Schafer, R. Murray. 1971. *The New Soundscape.* London: Universal Edition.

Schmitz, Hermann. 1969. *System der Philosophie,* vol. 3, book 2, *Der Gefühlsraum.* Bonn: Bouvier.

Sieden, Lloyd Steven. 1989. *Buckminster Fuller's Universe: His Life and Work.* Cambridge, MA: Perseus Publishing.

Sloterdijk, Peter. 1999. *Sphären II. Globen: Makrosphärologie.* Frankfurt am Main: Suhrkamp.

Sloterdijk, Peter. 2004. *Sphären III. Schäume: Plurale Sphärologie.* Frankfurt am Main: Suhrkamp.

Sloterdijk, Peter. 2008. 'Foam City', *Distinktion* 16: 47–59.

Sloterdijk, Peter. 2011. *Spheres, Volume I: Bubbles: Microspherology,* translated by Wieland Hoban. Los Angeles: Semiotext(e).

Zumthor, Peter. 2006. *Atmospheres: Architectural Environments – Surrounding Objects.* Basel, Boston, and Berlin: Birkhäuser Verlag.

**Atmospheres,
Art, Architecture**

**A Conversation
between Gernot
Böhme, Christian
Borch, Olafur
Eliasson & Juhani
Pallasmaa**

The Notion of Atmospheres

Christian Borch (CB): I would like to begin by addressing the notion of atmospheres. How did the interest in this concept emerge?

Gernot Böhme (GB): In a way, the notion of and interest in atmospheres came about as a reaction to modernity, where the orientation was much more towards geometry, technology, and the industrial production of buildings. In philosophy, and more specifically in phenomenology, the concept gained prominence through the work of Hermann Schmitz, for whom the term was mainly related to a theory of perception. Schmitz was inspired by, among others, the psychiatrist Hubert Tellenbach, who wrote a book on taste, smell, and atmosphere, *Geschmack und Atmosphäre* (Tellenbach 1968). In it, Tellenbach discussed the smell of the nest, the feeling and smell of the home, and the possible psychic disturbances that may arise if you lose the sense of smell. This forms part of the background for the phenomenological interest in atmospheres. But Schmitz also drew on Rudolph Otto and his idea of the numinous, i.e. the godlike powers that overcome us. Indeed, in Schmitz's work, atmospheres are mainly conceived of as things that overcome you. Therefore, his approach is much closer to a theory of the aesthetics of perception. For him, atmospheres are more or less feelings in the air.

I took another route, focusing on the *production of atmospheres.* In that sense, my work is complementary to Schmitz's. My central argument is that atmospheres are not only numinous, they are also produced by us, and there are professions whose very task it is to produce them. As a result, for me the art of stage-setting became the paradigm for the production of atmospheres, an attempt that you can also find in architecture, marketing, and various strategies of design, as well as in the stage-setting of commodities.

Juhani Pallasmaa (JP): This stage-setting is also identifiable in specific situations, for example in funeral halls and wedding venues.

CB: Yes – here too, stages are set for dramas to unfold.

Olafur Eliasson, *Beauty,* 1993. Installation view from *Minding the world,* ARoS Aarhus Kunstmuseum, Aarhus, DK, 2004.

JP: I have mainly used atmospheric thinking, in the sense in which atmosphere is understood when referring to the weather. But I think the notion of atmospheres is in balance with my understanding of the body image, or the embodied image, in its comprehensive, sudden grasping of the emotional and existential essence of a situation, whether social or architectural. And I think it is an important notion that should be taken seriously in architectural training.

Olafur Eliasson (OE): Like the weather, atmospheres change all the time and that's what makes the concept so important. An atmosphere cannot be an autonomous state; it cannot be in standstill, frozen. Atmospheres are productive, they are active agents. When you introduce atmosphere into a space, it becomes a reality machine.

If you talk about an atmosphere in public space, you can describe it as the coming together of numerous trajectories, the coming together of materials, of intentions, the buildings; it's a hovering, a resonance. It never stands still. It moves on and changes. The idea of atmospheres that is dominant today sometimes suggests that aesthetics are separate from ethics. But when we talk about atmospheres, especially in public space, we cannot take away intentionality. And intentions – by city planners, governments, everyday users – inevitably embody an ethical stance, a suggestion about how to act and interact with others.

CB: Gernot, you said that the interest in atmospheres should be seen as a reaction to modernity. Yet it also seems to me that the notion carries romantic undertones. For example, doesn't your reference to ruination in your essay endow the notion of atmospheres with a romantic aura, Juhani?

JP: I don't mean it that way. It refers to an iconic recognition of a weathered building, and clearly the weathering of a building indicates temporality. You could also say that it is a kind of exposure of vulnerability. The ruin even has such a strong, iconic place in the idea of time itself. The words 'romantic' and 'Romanticism' usually convey a disparaging or sentimental tone, but the era of Romanticism in the nineteenth century produced significant thinking in philosophy, psychology, and aesthetic theories.

Olafur Eliasson, *Green river*, 1998. Installation view in Stockholm, Sweden, 2000.

CB: One thing is to describe atmospheres from a phenomenological point of view, studying how we experience architecture. Another is to argue that atmospheres should form a kind of yardstick that architects should always keep in mind and measure their work against. Do you think that the notion of atmospheres entails such a normative dimension? That is, ought architects to consider the atmospheric dimension of their work? Should they even try to produce particular atmospheres, or would that become too much of a manipulative enterprise?

CB: I don't think the notion of atmospheres is a normative concept. But I do think it is about time that architects were far more aware of the role they play in producing atmospheres.

OE: When we speak about normativity and atmospheres, I think it is important to note that we are often numb to the atmospheres that surround us. Here, architectural detail and artistic intervention can make people more aware of an already existing atmosphere. That is, materiality can actually make atmospheres explicit – it can draw your attention and amplify your sensitivity to a particular atmosphere. All materials have psychosocial content, and the right material can make the atmosphere apparent by giving it a trajectory, by making it almost tangible. Yet it could also go another way: the materiality of something has the capacity to work in a non-normative or liberating manner, opening up new ways of engaging with the atmosphere.

Time and Space
CB: Your installation *The mediated motion* (2001) at Kunsthaus Bregenz, Austria (designed by Peter Zumthor) included interventions aimed at showing and producing different modes of behaviour than those usually made available by the building ('lines of flight', as Gilles Deleuze would call them), and in which temporality and movement would become means of challenging the atmosphere. Would this installation amount to the kind of non-normative capacity of the intervention in the atmosphere you just spoke about?

OE: Yes, I would say so, because temporality is by definition internal. I don't take it for granted that the sequence of experiences my body goes through when I move through a particular space will be the same for other people. But although I have a different 'time' from other people, I can also put myself in the position of the other. Phenomenology introduced the great idea that you can stand by a river and consider a boat as it is heading towards you. Then it is in front of you, and then, soon after, it has sailed further down the river. But I am also able to put myself in the time-construct of being on the boat, of seeing the landscape pass by me. And when walking through a building, I can actually elaborate on the construct of time to understand where I am in the building with regard to how I experience it temporally. So time is not a constant in that sense. I am psychologically capable of negotiating myself, my feeling of passage or sequence.

**A Conversation
between Gernot
Böhme, Christian
Borch, Olafur
Eliasson & Juhani
Pallasmaa**

CB: How would you see the temporal aspect of atmospheres, Gernot? It seems to me that, while Olafur emphasises how time and space interact, your interest revolves more around the strictly spatial dimension.

GB: That is true. I conceive of atmospheres as spaces. This may also be a definition of atmospheres: they are spaces with a mood, or emotionally felt spaces. This is an important definition, because it underlines that emotions do not always have to be in your heart or in your soul, something internal. Emotions can be on the outside, they can strike you. For example, a room can be filled with certain emotions. This is why I stress the spatial character of atmospheres. Atmospheres are, in a sense, entities – or 'quasi-things', as Schmitz termed them. They can creep, swell, and ebb. Weather atmospheres are an example of this: a thunderstorm is approaching, the weather is dark, and you really feel it coming nearer. So atmosphere is also a concept through which you are able to identify certain natural phenomena that are not really a subject of the natural sciences. What you need is a sort of phenomenology of nature in order to address the atmospheres of autumn, spring, or summer. This is nature as felt experience, but it is not just something objective. Similarly, the different times of the day, such as early morning or afternoon, have certain

Olafur Eliasson and Günther Vogt, *The mediated motion,* 2001. Installation view at Kunsthaus Bregenz, Austria, 2001.

Olafur Eliasson and Günther Vogt, *The mediated motion,* 2001. Installation view at
Kunsthaus Bregenz, Austria, 2001.

atmospheres. Descriptions of them are mostly found in literature, in poetry in particular. This is why I make use of literature to explain what these natural atmospheres are like. And, at least in this realm, the temporal dimension comes in too. Therefore I also sometimes talk about *the atmospheric,* to emphasise atmosphere as an entity out there, in terms of the stages of something coming ever closer.

JP: I find it interesting that you use 'atmospheric' as an adjective. Indeed, one might consider whether atmosphere is a noun or an adjective. I, for one, believe that certain fundamental architectural experiences are verbs rather than nouns. Architecture suggests or invites activities. In my view, a door is not architecture, whereas passing through a doorway, crossing the threshold between two realms, is a genuine architectural experience. Similarly, a window in itself is not yet architecture; it is the act of looking through the window, or of light falling in, that turns it into a meaningful architectural experience.

Capitalism
CB: In some of your work, Gernot, in particular your book *Architektur und Atmosphäre,* you reflect on the connection between capitalism and architecture. Could you elaborate on this connection?

GB: Yes, this is part of my critique of the way we live today. I follow Herbert Marcuse and others in saying that, since the 1950s, we in the Western hemisphere and in Japan have been living in affluent societies. This means that the essential demands of the people can easily be met, but that the market would be satisfied or would come to an end if only fundamental demands were met. To keep capitalism going, and not only going, but also growing, you must therefore extend the realm of the market. In German, I distinguish between *Bedürfnisse* and *Begehrnisse.* The first type is: you are thirsty, then you drink and the thirst is gone. The other type is: you meet the demand, then the demand is lifted to a higher level and becomes open-ended. I assert that the affluent society goes hand in hand with this extension of the fundamental demands.

**Atmospheres,
Art, Architecture**

**A Conversation
between Gernot
Böhme, Christian
Borch, Olafur
Eliasson & Juhani
Pallasmaa**

This relates to atmospheres because, in this type of economy, which is now aptly called the aesthetic economy, production increasingly shifts to an aestheticisation of life by means of art, design, and so on. Most of the demands created in the open-ended market are aesthetic demands. Following Marx, it makes sense to differentiate between the use-value and the market-value of a commodity, and to argue that many commodities are bought not because of their use-value but because of the design or stage-setting of the buyer that they offer. Put differently, this type of economy is an aesthetical economy, because the primary function of most of its products is to design and stage-set the person who buys them.

CB: How would you see connections between architecture, art, and atmospheres on the one side and capitalism on the other, Olafur?

OE: I agree that production in the West especially has become a production of aesthetics, and that even production itself has become aesthetic, as it is related to corporate brands. But I think we should not fail to acknowledge that conventional production, the manufacturing of everything else, is actually still taking place; it has just been moved elsewhere, to Asia and Africa, for example. So we have an aesthetic production in the so-called global North, and a kind of non-aesthetic production, which has been removed from our sight, in the less resourceful South. I agree that excess – the brutality of this excess – presents us with new existential challenges because we are not willing to give it up. There is very little reflection on this excess, and criticism of it is rarely translated into real action. I think we lack the necessary sensitivity to understand the consequences of the way we are living.

This also has atmospheric dimensions, which has become most explicit, during my lifetime, in respect of the climate, where there is obviously a link to consumption and excess. The world is trying to grasp these causal contracts with the climate. Here, we first have to acknowledge that the climate is in fact relative. When I was young, we all still assumed that the climate was a constant, that it was something outside of human reach. Now, we understand that the climate is not something natural but something cultural; we are co-responsible for it and we have to manage our

Olafur Eliasson and Günther Vogt, *The mediated motion,* 2001. Installation view at Kunsthaus Bregenz, Austria, 2001.

**Atmospheres,
Art, Architecture**

**A Conversation
between Gernot
Böhme, Christian
Borch, Olafur
Eliasson & Juhani
Pallasmaa**

own climate. This presents us with a great conflict, since we have our excessive lifestyle on the one hand, and our responsibility for dealing with the climate crisis on the other. Of course, I am oversimplifying. But if we can understand how we produce the climate and how the climate produces us – if we can understand the relationship we have with the climate – then we can also start to develop a sense of responsibility, a felt feeling of responsibility.

JP: I have in some of my lectures used the notion of mental ecology, for the reason that there is so much purely technologically oriented ecological thinking in architecture. This is really just a way of adding to the kind of machines and devices that we already have. We really need new ways of *thinking* and new ethical values before we can become effective enough. We need to grasp the primary processes and causalities in our culture and lifestyle, such as the constant and deliberate expansion of needs or desires that Gernot and Olafur spoke of. At present, we are trying to continue the unfeasible culture of perpetual growth and expansion by inventing new mechanisms to manage the negative and increasingly fatal consequences of our unreasonable aspirations. Many indigenous cultures, such as that of the Native Americans, exemplify a sustainable ethics of life. Today, biophilia, 'the science and love of life', promoted by Edward O. Wilson, is an attempt to formulate the parameters of an ecologically reasonable human culture. One of the main issues is the dilemma that Erich Fromm pointed out in the 1960s, namely the one between having rather than being, measuring quality of life through possession rather than authentic experience.

Politics
CB: These references to responsibility and new ways of thinking also point to the domain of politics. How do you see the relations between politics and atmospheres?

GB: Well, first of all, I feel that as a philosopher I must remain critical of what is taking place. For example, I have studied historical phenomena such as Nazi architecture, the architecture of Albert Speer and the orchestration of big mass movements during and between the world wars. Today,

I feel that my critical task has to be directed towards all sorts of contemporary mass meetings – in sports, popular music, etc. – and to consider whether they have a comparable function in our society. What appears to me is that the current mass formations are surprisingly apolitical, as younger people in particular seem to gather around non-political issues. This is quite different to most of the twentieth century. Another interest of mine is the staging of atmospheres in the commercial field, in shopping malls, for instance. In practice, I study how such atmospheres are organised by taking photos of malls and recording their soundscapes.

CB: How about you, Juhani, do you see any connection to the political domain, or notions of resistance, or do they somehow seem to be of less importance for you in a discussion of atmospheres?

JP: No, I think they are very essential. I see the artist's task, as well as that of the architect, very much in terms of resistance. In Finnish, we have a saying: 'doing the mole's work', i.e. building tunnels underground. When I was the architect for the biggest project in the history of Helsinki, in the city centre, I felt like a mole in the sense that I had to introduce, convey, safeguard, and, more importantly, keep quiet about major issues that concerned the society as a whole, such as the impact, meaning, and character of the atmospheres of public spaces, and the invisible message and power of architecture. It is really frightening how little, if at all, the political decision-makers and authorities care about the fundamental societal tasks of architecture. In the Helsinki project I just referred to, not one municipal committee asked a question or made a remark about the public space and the symbolic or atmospheric impact of the project. Everyone was concerned with costs, timetables, and even window cleaning! I find it rather remarkable that – in many important tasks – the architect is left completely alone to defend the traditional values of architecture. Architecture used to be about mediating between macro-cosmos and micro-cosmos, it was the art of mediation. Today, it is the art of investment!

The other political aspect that I find important is the element of idealisation. I don't believe that meaningful architecture can arise from answering the explicit demands or desires of clients or society at large.

Atmospheres of globalisation. Addis Ababa, Ethiopia, 2011.

The cultural level has to be slightly elevated, otherwise there is no developing culture. So I see idealisation as an essential element in both the artistic sphere and the architectural world. And again, that requires the courage to defend something that nobody else cares about – in other words, 'this is what the society could become if things were different'. In the current strand of global capitalism, the architect usually has to work quietly, not saying what he or she really means.

'Only if poets and writers set themselves tasks that no one else dares imagine will literature continue to have a function', writes Italo Calvino in his *Six Memos for the Next Millennium* (Calvino 1988: 112). He adds, '[m]y confidence in the future of literature consists in the knowledge that there are things that only literature can give us' (1988: front matter). I think that the future of architecture as a profound, humanly, and culturally significant activity relies on the very same demands.

CB: How do other architects look upon that? I suppose not all architects share your point of view; some are more instrumental in their approach.

JP: Of course. There are a huge number of architects who see architecture as a rationalised technology, an instrumental utility, a matter of aesthetics or even business. I have always been disturbed by these ideas. I think architecture is too deeply existential and too deeply collective to become anybody's business; it has to be something else. But I know it is a minority view.

OE: I agree that heightened cultural sensitivity is essential. I think another challenge is to understand the conditions under which we do this – and more specifically, to understand that every time we come up with a solution to raise the cultural bar, it can only be the solution for that particular moment and that particular place and context. We should be careful not to suggest that what is important about architecture can be transferred elsewhere as a system of truth, to suppose that we have found out what is right and wrong and then simply duplicate it. We also need to find a way of raising the cultural bar with very little resources, with a few corrugated metal plates and a couple of wooden sticks, for example.

In other words, the challenge is to work with limited resources, or almost no resources at all, to suggest a cultural upgrade that might simply pave the way for more fundamental grassroots establishments, which might in turn give rise to a new beginning for society.

JP: I just want to add one sentence to what you said. The possibility of political architecture growing is much greater on a smaller scale and with reduced resources than in large-scale projects with huge budgets, because in the latter case other agendas will always enter and destroy the political agenda. So in that sense I would say that architects are bound to seek more humane architecture under rather humble conditions. And that is exactly what is now happening. There is a lot of very fine political architecture – one-family houses and small structures – around the world, but in the magazines we see only big projects. As we are speaking here about atmospheres, we need to acknowledge that traditional vernacular architectures, arising from local conditions, materials, and skills, are often highly atmospheric. Even in today's world, an architecture that is regionally and culturally rooted creates appealing atmospheres, as opposed to the placeless globalism of our current industrial and consumerist culture.

References

Calvino, Italo. 1988.
Six Memos for the Next Millennium: The Charles Eliot Norton lectures, 1985–86. Cambridge, MA: Harvard University Press.

Tellenbach, Hubert. 1968.
Geschmack und Atmosphäre: Medien menschlichen Elementarkontaktes. Salzburg: Otto Müller.

Olafur Eliasson, *Din blinde passager,* 2010. Installation view at ARKEN Museum for Moderne Kunst, 2010.

Contributors

Gernot Böhme is Professor Emeritus of Philosophy at Darmstadt Technical University and Director of the Institute for Practical Philosophy, e.V., Ipph, in Darmstadt, Germany. Böhme has a background in mathematics, physics, and philosophy, and he has published seminal work in a variety of fields, covering everything from the work of classical philosophers such as Plato and Aristotle to philosophical anthropology and ethics, nature, aesthetics, time, etc. Böhme's key works on atmospheres are *Atmosphäre. Essays zur neuen Ästhetik* (Suhrkamp, 7th ed. 2013); *Anmutungen. Über das Atmosphärische* (Edition Tertium, 1998); and *Architektur und Atmosphäre* (Wilhelm Fink, 2nd ed. 2013).

Christian Borch is Professor of Political Sociology at the Department of Management, Politics, and Philosophy, Copenhagen Business School, Denmark. His research focuses on crowds, architecture, financial markets, urban theory, power, and criminology. He has published widely on these issues as well as on key social theorists such as Gabriel Tarde, Niklas Luhmann, and Peter Sloterdijk. Recent books include *Soziologie der Nachahmung und des Begehrens. Materialien zu Gabriel Tarde* (Suhrkamp, 2009; edited with Urs Stäheli); *Niklas Luhmann (Key Sociologists)* (Routledge, 2011); and *The Politics of Crowds: An Alternative History of Sociology* (Cambridge University Press, 2012). He is co-founder and editor-in-chief of *Distinktion: Scandinavian Journal of Social Theory.*

Olafur Eliasson is a Danish-Icelandic artist. Eliasson incessantly explores our modes of perceiving. His work spans photography, installation, sculpture, and film. In 2003, he represented Denmark at the 50th Venice Biennale and installed *The weather project* at Tate Modern, London. The 2007 SFMOMA exhibition *Take your time: Olafur Eliasson* toured until 2010. Projects in public space include *Green river,* staged in various cities between 1998 and 2001; the Serpentine Gallery Pavilion 2007, London, with Kjetil Thorsen; and *The New York City Waterfalls,* 2008. Recent architectural works include *Your rainbow panorama,* for ARoS Aarhus Kunstmuseum, and Harpa Reykjavik Concert Hall and Conference Centre, with Henning Larsen Architects.

Juhani Pallasmaa is one of Finland's most distinguished architects and architectural thinkers. His previous positions include: Rector of the Institute of Industrial Arts, Helsinki; Director of the Museum of Finnish Architecture, Helsinki; and Professor and Dean of the Faculty of Architecture, Helsinki University of Technology. He has also held visiting professorships at several universities around the world. Pallasmaa is the author/editor of thirty books, including *The Eyes of the Skin: Architecture and the Senses* (Academy, 1995, and John Wiley & Sons, 2005); *The Thinking Hand: Existential and Embodied Wisdom in Architecture* (John Wiley & Sons, 2009); and *The Embodied Image: Imagination and Imagery in Architecture* (John Wiley & Sons, 2011).

Index

Photo Credits p. 9 Natalie Tepper / Arcaid / Corbis **pp. 10, 17, 67, 69** Jeanne Fredac
pp. 14, 63, 64, 70 Digital image courtesy of the Getty's Open Content Program **p. 23**
Courtesy of Galerie van Gelder, Amsterdam **p. 25** Turner Bequest, 1856, The National
Gallery, London **p. 28** Tate, London 2014 **pp. 31, 36** Rauno Träskelin **p. 33** Hélène Binet
pp. 44–57 Gernot Böhme **p. 74** Henri Bureau / Sygma / Corbis **p. 76** Hulton-Deutsch
Collection / Corbis **pp. 79, 83** Hans Wilschut **pp. 84, 87, 94, 107** Studio Olafur
Eliasson **p. 92** Poul Pedersen **pp. 97–101** Markus Tretter **p. 104** Christian Borch
Cover Olafur Eliasson, *Double sunset*, 1999; photo: Hans Wilschut.

 With the kind support of the Dreyer Foundation

Editor Christian Borch
Texts Gernot Böhme, Christian Borch, Olafur Eliasson, Juhani Pallasmaa
Copy editing Tam McTurk, Keonaona Peterson
Project management Alexander Felix, Petra Schmid
Layout, cover design and typography Jenna Gesse

Library of Congress Cataloging-in-Publication Data
A CIP catalog record for this book has been applied for at the Library of Congress.

Bibliographic information published by the German National Library
The German National Library lists this publication in the Deutsche Nationalbiblio-
grafie; detailed bibliographic data are available on the Internet at http://dnb.dnb.de.

© 2014 Birkhäuser Verlag GmbH, Basel
P.O. Box 44, 4009 Basel, Switzerland
Part of De Gruyter

Printed on acid-free paper produced from chlorine-free pulp. TCF ∞

Printed in Germany
ISBN 978-3-03821-512-7

9 8 7 6 5 4 3 2 1   www.birkhauser.com